DANIEL GRAY is a manuscripts curator in the National Library of Scotland. He is a graduate of Newcastle University. His first book, *The Historical Dictionary of Marxism* (Scarecrow Press), was published in 2007. Gray has worked as a researcher, contributor and writer on BBC radio and on STV's 2-part documentary series *The Scots Who Fought Franco*. He has also written on football for *When Saturday Comes* and *Fly me to the Moon*, the fanzine of his beloved Middlesbrough FC. He is married to Marisa and lives in Edinburgh.

Praise for *Homage to Caledonia*

Daniel Gray has done a marvellous job in bringing together the stories of Scots volunteers... in [this] many-voiced, multi-layered book. SCOTLAND ON SUNDAY

[Gray] has organised a complex story into a well-constructed and compelling narrative. He can write – his prose is unfussy, fluent and warm. Best of all, he has squared the circle of producing accurate history while retaining a deep respect for the men and women who people it... moving and thought-provoking. THE HERALD

Excellent... highly effective. THE SCOTS MAGAZINE

A new and fascinating contribution. SCOTTISH REVIEW OF BOOKS

Excellent... a rigorous, well written and entertaining assessment of Scotland's contribution to that chapter of European history. Jamie Hepburn MSP, HOLYROOD MAGAZINE

Book of the week... Gray deserves applause for shining a light on a lesser-known aspect of the nation's character of which we should all be proud. PRESS AND JOURNAL

A very human history of the conflict emerges. SCOTTISH FIELD

The latest addition to a line of excellent books detailing the efforts of British men and women in Spain. MORNING STAR

Homage to Caledonia

Scotland and the Spanish Civil War

DANIEL GRAY

Luath Press Limited

EDINBURGH

www.luath.co.uk

First published 2008
Reprinted 2009
This edition 2009

ISBN: 978-1-906817-16-9

The author's right to be identified as author of this book
under the Copyright, Designs and Patents Act 1988 has been asserted.

The paper used in this book is recyclable.
It is made from low-chlorine pulps produced in a low-energy,
low-emission manner from renewable forests.

Printed in the UK by
CPI Mackays, Chatham ME5 8TD

Typeset in 10.5 point Sabon

Map © Neil Gower

Published in association with

National Library
of Scotland

www.nls.uk

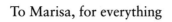

To Marisa, for everything

Picture it. The Calton. Fair Fortnight. 1937. Full of Eastern Promise. Wimmen windaehingin. Weans greetin for pokey hats. Grown men, well intae their hungry thirties, slouchin at coarners, skint as a bairn's knees. The sweet smell of middens, full and flowing over in the sun. Quick! There's a scramble in Parnie Street! The wee yin there's away wae a hauf-croon.

Back closes runnin wae dug pee and East End young team runnin wae the San Toy, the Kent Star, the Sally Boys, the Black Star, the Calton Entry Mob, the Cheeky Forty, the Romeo Boys, the Antique Mob, and the Sticklit Boys. Then there wiz the Communist Party. Red rags tae John Bull. But if things wur bad in the Calton they wur worse elsewhere. Franco in the middle. Mussolini oan the right-wing. Hitler waitin tae come oan. When they three goat thegither an came up against the Spanish workers, they didnae expect the Calton to offer handers.

The heirs a John MacLean, clutchin a quire a *Daily Workers*, staunin oan boaxes at the Green, shakin thur fists at the crowds that gathered tae hear aboot the plight ae the Spanish Republic. Oot ae these getherins oan the Green came the heroes ae the International Brigade, formin the front line against fascism.

The Blackshirts, the Brownshirts, the Blueshirts, fascists of every colour an country came up against the men an women ae no mean city, against grey simmets an bunnets an headscarfs, against troosers tied wae string an shoes that let the rain in, against guns that were auld enough tae remember Waterloo. Fae nae hair tae grey hair they answered the call. Many never came back. They wur internationalists. They wur Europeans. They wur Scots. Glasgow should be proud ae them!

From the Calton to Catalonia, John and Willy Maley

Contents

Foreword

Daniel Gray's important and powerful book *Homage to Caledonia* tells the story of those deeply committed and courageous Scots who volunteered to fight for democracy and socialism against General Franco and his forces – backed by Hitler and Mussolini – in the Spanish Civil War against an elected Republican Government.

The British establishment was openly sympathetic to the fascists, and its policy of 'non-intervention' was known on the left to be their way to stay clear so that Franco could win, but the left in Scotland rallied to the cause and apart from those who actually fought and died there, there was a great campaign to raise money and support.

As a teenager, I wrote a school essay in support of the republicans and against Franco on which my teacher wrote a one-word comment, 'Disgusting', so that told me a lot about him.

That war can be seen as a prelude to the second world war, and if Franco had been defeated, Europe might have escaped the horrors of 1939–45.

This book is very timely because the economic chaos that led to fascism seems to be threatening again today in the so-called 'credit crunch', which should remind us that the left has always to be vigilant.

Tony Benn, October 2008

Acknowledgements

I have been stimulated and encouraged by the kind help and knowledge of widows, sons, daughters and nieces of those who participated in the Spanish Civil War. In particular, David Drever, Annie Dunlop, Sandra Elders, Alan Murray, Sonna Murray, Sheila Stuart, Liz Pettie, and George and Nan Park all offered me stories, wisdom, and copious amounts of tea, cakes and soup. The words of Willy Maley were almost as great a motivation as the actions of his father. I am grateful, too, for their cooperation in allowing me to use the letters and archives of their relatives. Mike Arnott, Jim Carmody and Marlene Sidaway of the International Brigades Memorial Trust have been enormously helpful. Ian MacDougall's written and spoken words have been of immense value, as has been the advice of Richard Baxell, Alan Warren and Don Watson. A grant from the Strathmartine Trust facilitated an extremely useful study trip to Spain.

Thanks are due to David Higham Associates for permission to use a quote from Muriel Spark's *The Prime of Miss Jean Brodie*. The unendingly patient and obliging Dr John Callow of the Marx Memorial Library deserves special praise, and thanks for permission to use quotes from the library's International Brigades archive. Images and quotes appear courtesy of private collections belonging to the relatives of International Brigaders, and holdings of the National Library of Scotland (see Archival Sources, page 213). Photographs of the Scottish Ambulance Unit originally appeared in the *Glasgow Evening Herald*. Every effort has been made to trace the copyright holders of material reproduced in the book. In case of any query, please contact the publisher.

At the National Library of Scotland, Maria Castrillo, Kenneth Dunn, Lauren Forbes, Cate Newton, Stephen Rigden, Robin Smith and Chris Taylor have been supportive in the extreme. Special thanks go to my translator Elena Fresco Barreira, the only Spaniard I know who uses the word 'ken'. Gavin MacDougall has made Luath Press the ideal publishing house to write for, as well as supplying some outstanding ideas for the book, including the title. The support of his colleague Leila Cruickshank has also been invaluable, as has the assiduous work and treasured advice of my editor Jennie Renton.

The opinions expressed in *Homage to Caledonia* are those of the author and not of the publisher or any institution.

On a personal level, my mum and dad's encouragement continues to know no bounds, and I cannot give thanks enough for the faith shown in me by Marisa, first a football widow, and lately a Spanish Civil War widow. Finally, my greatest, sadly posthumous, thanks must go to Steve Fullarton: quite simply, an inspiration.

Chronology of Events

1926 General Strike, in which many future International Brigaders participated.
1931 April: Second Spanish Republic proclaimed and reform programme instigated.
1932 Inauguration of Oswald Mosley's British Union of Fascists.
1933 November: victory for right-wing parties in Spanish general election. Halt of reform programme.
1934 Fifth National Hunger March to London.
1936 February to June: Popular Front administration elected in Spain. Government of Manuel Azaña recommence and extend reform programme, exile military leaders, and ban the Falange Española.
       12–13 July: José Castillo, then José Calvo Sotelo killed in Madrid.
       17–18 July: Generals' military uprising launched from Spanish Morocco.
       20 July onwards: Hitler and Mussolini begin to supply the nationalists with military aid, while the Comintern agrees to help establish the International Brigades.
       4 August 1936: the British and French governments sign Non-Intervention Treaty.
       September onwards: Britain and major powers formally commit to non-intervention in Spain. Large numbers of volunteers begin to arrive to fight for the republicans, contributing to the defence of Madrid and assault on Lopera. In Britain, members of the National Unemployed Workers' Movement march on London. Many future International Brigaders from Scotland participate.
       October: republicans begin to receive military aid from the Soviet Union.
1937 January: Foreign Enlistment Act invoked in Britain. British Battalion formed in Spain.
       February: British Battalion take part in their first battle, at the Jarama Valley.
       April: nationalist bombing of Guernica
       May: Barcelona street-fighting.
       June: Death of Bob Smillie.
       July: British Battalion participate in the Battle of Brunete.
       August: British Battalion transferred to the Aragon Front, and help to capture Quinto and Belchite.
       October: British Battalion's disastrous assault on Fuentes de Ebro.

December: British Battalion participate in the Aragon offensive and capture of Teruel.

1938 January: British Battalion eventually succumb to the nationalist invasion of Teruel. From March, republicans retreat through Aragon, and Franco's troops reach the Mediterranean, dissecting the Spanish republic.

July: British Battalion cross back over the River Ebro and participate in republican offensive.

21 September: Juan Negrin announces the withdrawal of international volunteers from the republican army.

28 October: British Battalion take part in parade of honour through the streets of Barcelona.

December: British Battalion members begin to arrive home.

1939 February: British government recognises Franco as Spain's sovereign leader.

1 April: nationalist victory complete.

1 September: Hitler invades Poland; beginning of World War Two.

THE STAGES OF THE SPANISH CIVIL WAR

FRANCE

FERROL
OVIEDO
BILBAO
HENDAYE
2
GUERNICA
PERPIGNAN

VIGO
BURGOS
1
SARAGOSSA

PORTUGAL

SALAMANCA
BELCHITE
3
BARCELONA

MADRID
2
TERUEL
MALLORCA
2

TOLEDO
CASTELLÓN

VALENCIA

BADAJOZ
CASTUERA
2
ALBACETE
IBIZA
2

ALICANTE

1
SEVILLE
1
GRANADA
CARTAGENA

MALAGA

TANGIER
CEUTA
TETOUAN
MELILLA

CANARY
ISLANDS
1

CASABLANCA
SPANISH
MOROCCO

1	Nationalist controlled territory July 1936
2	Nationalist gains by October 1937
3	Nationalist gains by July 1938

0   MILES   200

JULY, 1936 — JULY, 1938

Introduction

One of Joyce Emily's boasts was that her brother at Oxford had gone to fight in the Spanish Civil War. This dark, rather mad girl wanted to go too, and to wear a white blouse and black skirt and march with a gun. Nobody had taken this seriously. The Spanish Civil War was something going on outside in the newspapers and only once a month in the school debating society. Everyone, including Joyce Emily, was anti-Franco if they were anything at all.

The Prime of Miss Jean Brodie, Muriel Spark

ON 7 MARCH 2008, under a leaden sky, several hundred people gathered in homage to the final survivor of a proud yet largely overlooked episode in Scotland's history. Of 549 Scots who fought in the Spanish Civil War, Steve Fullarton was the last to die, adding a weight of poignancy to the sombre mood of those present at Warriston Crematorium, Leith. With him had gone Caledonia's final active link to a conflict that defined the lives of an entire generation of Scots: it was in the Spanish Civil War, whether they participated directly or not, that their own struggles became embodied.

Documenting a selection of individual narratives, *Homage to Caledonia* brings Scotland's contribution to events in Spain into focus: by showing not only the role of Scots in Spain but also the way in which the conflict impacted on life in Scotland, the book sets out to explain how and why this became Scotland's war. It is a social history rather than a military one and is not intended to be a comprehensive history of the battles, politics and intricacies of the wider Spanish Civil War.

Reaction to hostilities in Spain must be viewed through the prism of 1930s Scotland; in the context of this highly politicised era, it is possible to appreciate why support for the republican government was so unequivocal. Popular modern perceptions of, for instance, communism are invalid, and hindsight largely irrelevant. The thirties were a time of intense idealism, of faith in democracy, anti-fascism and often of fealty to the Soviet Union, her atrocious excesses and distortions as yet unrecognised by most. More than obeisance to political dogma though, it was a time of sheer hope; a better tomorrow could be won through collective action, not just in Scotland, but in Spain too. To the Scottish working class, the struggles of the 1930s were the same struggles whether in Buckhaven or Barcelona. It is no coincidence that many of the Scots who fought in Spain referred to themselves as internationalists.

For many people, the primary impression of Scotland's relationship with the Spanish Civil War has come from Muriel Spark's *The Prime of Miss Jean Brodie*, in which a schoolgirl, Joyce Emily Hammond, travels to fight for Franco as a response to the fascistic, doctrinaire education she receives from the book's eponymous teacher. Joyce Emily is killed before witnessing any action: even in the insular bourgeois world of a conservative Edinburgh girls' school, the Spanish Civil War in all its brutal colour could not be avoided.

The Scottish people responded with alacrity to the coup d'état launched by General Francisco Franco and his cabal of supporters on 18 July 1936. That coup was both the culmination of years of simmering tensions, and the trigger for a fierce war involving troops from across Europe; truly, it was Spain's Archduke Franz Ferdinand moment.

Spain in the 1930s was a land of schisms between monarchists and republicans, Catholics and those opposed to the social, political and economic power of the church, and feudal landowners and peasants. That latter group, impoverished and largely illiterate, made up a substantial proportion of the Spanish population and constituted the main support base of the reformist republican government, which was elected on 16 February 1936.

The new 'Popular Front' government of Manuel Azaña, a figure reviled by conservatives, monarchists and military leaders, recommenced a series of political and social reforms halted in 1933 by the election of a right-wing regime (the original reforms had been instigated in 1931 with the proclamation of the Second Spanish Republic, and had included the enfranchisement of women, the legalisation of divorce, a reduction of the military's size and influence, and the redistribution of feudal land amongst peasants). In a frenzied atmosphere of flux, new legislation was also introduced, enhancing the rights of peasants and penalising the landed aristocracy. Spain's reactionary establishment were outraged. Their ire was accentuated when the government sought to extinguish a threatened rebellion by exiling and isolating military chiefs including Franco, who was banished to Spanish Morocco. These actions heightened unrest among the government's opponents and, supported by the newly outlawed right-wing Falange party, Franco and his military cohorts Emilio Mola, Juan Yague and José Sanjurjo began plotting a coup.

In the summer of 1936, Spain reached breaking point. On 12 July, a left-wing police officer in Madrid, José Castillo, was murdered by a fascist group, creating an incendiary mood and rioting. The following day, the left took its revenge: José Calvo Sotelo, leader of the conservative opposition in the Spanish parliament, was killed by Luis Cuenca, a commando with the civilian police. Though it is doubtful that the Popular Front government ordered the assassination of Sotelo, the slaying of a man who had virulently protested against Azaña's reforms and openly admitted to being a fascist aroused the suspicions of the right, and exacerbated their feeling that an overthrow of the government was necessary. In this context, Franco and his henchmen launched their attack on the mainland from Ceuta in Spanish Morocco. Spain was at war.

The conspirators had anticipated a swift and comprehensive victory and, with the help of sympathetic army generals, were able to overrun swaths of southern Spain. They had not reckoned upon resistance from soldiers sympathetic to the republican cause and civilians fiercely protective of the elected government. Forming the republican side, an alliance of anarchists, communists, democrats, moderates, socialists and trade unionists sprang to the defence of that administration. Rather than conquering Spain rapidly and incisively, Franco and his nationalist army were left with isolated pockets of territory.

From the end of July, the nationalists began to receive significant military assistance from Adolf Hitler's Germany and Benito Mussolini's Italy. Crucially for the continuation of Franco's early assault, German planes were provided to facilitate the mass airlift of his elite Army of Africa from Morocco to mainland Spain. For their part, the republican side received foreign assistance in the form of the volunteers that flocked over their borders to form militias and eventually the International Brigades, and, from October, materiel and troops from the Soviet Union. Rather than a civil war, then, Spain's conflict became one of foreign intervention.

The Scottish desire to intervene was, in that sense, typical, though in its scale it was unique. Of the estimated 2,400 men and women who left Britain to serve in Spain, about 20 per cent were from Scotland. This is especially impressive when one considers that Scots then comprised only 10 per cent of the population of Great Britain. There were, too, Scottish volunteers from groups unaffiliated with the International Brigades, such as those who travelled to serve with the Independent Labour Party (ILP) contingent. The mass base of Scottish support for the Spanish republic, though, centred around the phenomenally successful 'Aid for Spain' movements, which garnered support across class, party and gender. In the Spanish cause, Scotland found a place to channel its energies, and the country's efforts outweighed those of any similarly populated area in Britain, or indeed the world.

PART I
From One Struggle to Another

CHAPTER I

Connecting the Fight:
Scotland in the 1930s

An empty stomach made an empty head think.

Tommy Bloomfield, Kirkcaldy

THE POLITICAL FIRES of 1930s Scotland burned and crackled unremittingly. Entertainment and education came from the soapbox oratory of radical street preachers; a truly open university. What a massive working class lacked in ha'pennies to rub together, it made up for with a bountiful grassroots democracy. Talking and listening on corners, men and women became inspired to struggle against poverty and fascism, domestic and foreign. Shortly before he passed away, Steve Fullarton described the often incendiary atmosphere in which future fellow International Brigader Jimmy Maley held court:

> I always attended his meetings. The Communist Party organiser would say 'it's time we had a meeting'. If Jimmy was available, he would always go. So Jimmy would carry this collapsible platform up to Shettleston Cross and I would give a hand to take it up there. Or, sometimes it was to help with chalking the streets, announcing that tomorrow night there would be a meeting by the Communist Party and Jimmy Maley would be speaking. Sometimes we painted it with whitewash; the traffic was such then that you could do that.
>
> Jimmy Maley was a provocative speaker. He knew that the Catholic young men would be there in force, repeating whatever lies had been issued to them from the chapel. They would come out with these ridiculous things, even too ridiculous to bother about. Jimmy would be right in there and would knock the feet from under them, would leave them speechless.

Their Scotland was one of communist councillors and Members of Parliament, and seemingly endless waves of strike action, protest marches, and demonstrations. Very early on in the Spanish war, this movement lent its categorical support to the republican side. When in August 1936 an Ayr businessman confirmed that he was refitting small aeroplanes to sell on to 'Spanish agents', 400 people turned up at a spontaneous protest meeting and

Kirkcaldy volunteer Tommy Bloomfield, right, with two fellow Brigaders.

passed a resolution demanding that none of the aircraft should end up in the hands of General Franco's forces. Around the same time, in Kirkcaldy sympathetic pilots dropped pro-republican leaflets on crowds attending a British Empire air display and 2,000 copies of the communist *Daily Worker*'s anti-Franco 'Spain Special' were sold in two hours on a Saturday night at Argyle Street, Glasgow.

Though home to a resilient and tenacious people, this seedbed of radicalism was afflicted by horrific levels of poverty and limited life expectancy: the Labour MP for Stirling, Tom Johnston, lamented that poor, slum-like housing had saddled Scotland with the highest death rate in northern Europe. Tommy Bloomfield of Kirkcaldy, who served two separate terms during the Spanish conflict, endured a life of crushing hardship familiar to many Scottish republican volunteers. Bloomfield worked from the age of 11, delivering milk and bread in the mornings and working evenings in a dance hall 'called the Bolshie, owing to the politics of the man who ran it'. Unemployed at 16, he 'obtained a job chipping the tar off casie sets at ninepence an hour. The contractor was so hard and greedy that if he saw you straightening your back, you were sacked.' It was in this context that many Scots turned to left-wing politics as a vehicle for their passage out of scarcity. As Bloomfield later remarked, 'An empty stomach made an empty head think.'

Members of the Scottish working class threw themselves from the dole queue and the soup kitchen into the maelstrom of progressive politics and all of the agitation and protest entailed therein. These were times of daily ferment and solidarity. In the first week of August 1936, 30,000 people marched against the government's new means test-based Unemployment Regulations in Lanarkshire, while protests took place in the name of the same cause in Leith, Greenock and Kelvingrove. Incredibly, Glasgow City Council *asked* its citizens to campaign against the Regulations, and in the Vale of Leven the council voted 17 to two in favour of protest. Clydeside Rivet Boys went out on strike in solidarity, then in September 54 miners at the Dickson Colliery in Blantyre began a stay-down strike over pay and conditions. When the authorities refused to send down food or water for the men, tens of thousands of Lanarkshire miners walked out on strike in sympathy. The following month, Caledonian rebellion crossed the border into England, as 2,000 Scottish fisher girls at Great Yarmouth staged a lightning strike against low pay. According to the *Daily Worker*, 'the girls suddenly threw down their gutting knives and rushed through the curing yards, their numbers growing as they shouted their demands'. The women were hosed down and restrained by police, their rebellion quashed, if not their spirits.

The protests of redundant workers were voiced most formally by the National Unemployed Workers' Movement (NUWM). In autumn 1936, the NUWM organised a hunger march from Scotland to London in protest at the proposed use of means testing. The march was completed by a number of men who would go on to fight in Spain. As Scottish NUWM leader Harry McShane suggested, 'many of them [marchers] understood the significance of the war, and some expressed the desire to fight in Spain for the republic'. One of them was Bob Cooney of Aberdeen, arrested for chalking slogans on to the road as the march passed through Dundee. On being bailed, Cooney vented his anger outside the police station:

> Apparently, chalking is illegal in this democratic city. The first intimation I had of this was when two limbs of the law swooped down on me and carried me off in a manner which suggested that they had got hold of Public Enemy Number One.

The 700 marchers, divided into east and west parties, regularly faced similar obfuscation from local authorities as they progressed south, though they were welcomed, fed and housed by compassionate locals throughout the country.

The Scottish contingent arrived in London on 8 November 1936 to participate in a national demonstration at Hyde Park attended by up to 100,000 people. Thirty Fife marchers were invited to take tea in the House of Commons with the East Fife Communist MP, Willie Gallacher, who consistently gave them solid support in parliament, fulminating against means testing and attacking Prime Minister Stanley Baldwin with the words, 'You preach humanity – let's have some of it.'

After a week of action in London, many of the Scottish marchers were firmly of the belief that poverty and the Spanish war were essentially facets of the same struggle. As well as Cooney, marchers like John Lennox of Aberdeen and Thomas Brannon of Blantyre started to conclude that they could influence this struggle most by making their way to Spain. The *Daily Worker* had already championed this theme a fortnight into Spain's war, beseeching readers to 'Smash the means test! Support the Spanish workers' fight for democracy!'

Underpinning these struggles ran a deep-seated antipathy to fascism, whether in Scotland or further afield. If, ran the consensus, fascism was not defeated in Spain, it would soon have to be defeated on an unknown and unparalleled scale at home instead; 'Bombs on Madrid today means bombs on London tomorrow' became a common slogan. The popular mood in Scotland was overwhelmingly anti-fascist, as was demonstrated by the outrage provoked when the Scottish Football Association arranged an October 1936 match against Germany at Ibrox Park, the home of Glasgow Rangers. In protest at the fixture, local William MacDonald summed up the mood when he wrote to the *Daily Worker*:

The Nazis have violated every law and rule of sportsmanship and decency, and yet they have the insolence to send a team of propagandists on to Glasgow, a socialist city noted for its love of freedom and democracy. There will be no football at Ibrox on that particular day: in the interests of peace and safety the magistrates of Glasgow should urge an entire veto of the match. In this they will have the loyal support of all lovers of peace and fair play. The Scottish people want no truck with the representatives of Hitler and von Papen. Our slogan and that of the trade unions should be: 'No truck with the Nazi murderers'. If an impudent attempt is made to proceed with the match, I can visualise in Glasgow the mightiest protest demonstration of our time.

Despite the objections of MacDonald and others, the match did go ahead, Scotland running out 2–0 victors. A number of anti-Nazi protesters were arrested, their fury amplified by the raising above the ground's main entrance of a swastika flag.

Archie Dewar, Bob Cooney and Bob Simpson, all Aberdonians who carried the anti-fascist fight from the streets of their home city to Spain.

Prior to fighting fascism in Spain, many Scottish volunteers were involved with domestic action against Oswald Mosley's British Union of Fascists (BUF). Key in the battle against fascism at home was the city of Aberdeen. There, a broad anti-fascist group, galvanised by opposition to the 1935 Italian invasion of Abyssinia, took hold with gusto.

Regular street meetings and demonstrations were held, with locals perhaps more acutely aware of British fascism than residents of other towns and cities, owing to the fact that Mosley's BUF leader in Scotland, William Chambers-Hunter, was a local resident. Chambers-Hunter was later to leave the BUF after Mosley became, in his eyes, 'too dictatorial', which suggests, to put it mildly, that he lacked political foresight when he agreed to work for the Hitler-admiring Englishman.

After pre-advertised meetings ended in their being driven from the streets, local fascists attempted on many occasions to hold spontaneous convocations in Aberdeen, but a network of cyclists, scouts and transport workers quickly spread the word, allowing the city's anti-fascists the chance to mobilise. As Bob Cooney remembered:

I felt we had to smash them off the streets. When the BUF arrived we'd shout 'These are the black-shirted bastards who are murdering kiddies in Spain – spit on them, kids.' Sometimes we'd be too late because the women had already dealt with them!

The link between Aberdeen and Spain manifested itself in local events shortly before the Spanish war began. An Iberian ship, the ss *Eolo*, docked in Aberdeen in early July 1936, its crew unaware that the reformist republican government in Madrid had decreed that all seamen should receive pay rises. Bob Cooney and local Communist councillor Tom Baxter boarded the *Eolo* to inform the crewmen of their rights. When the captain of the ship refused to grant the revised wages, the seamen immediately went on strike. They received support and gifts from local groups, and the Aberdeen Trades Council resolved to do all in their power to prevent a 'blackleg' crew being admitted onto the ship. After three months, the vessel was ordered back to Spain prompting tearful goodbyes on both sides.

One of those who fundraised for the crewmen was Aberdonian John Londragan, who later fought in Spain. In an amazing coincidence, while there, Londragan spotted a postcard of Aberdeen harbour in the window of a photography shop in a village near to Brunete. On enquiring, he was delighted and overwhelmed to find that the postcard had been sent home by a crewmember of the *Eolo* he had befriended, Juan Atturie.

Outside of Aberdeen, many other Scottish volunteers served their anti-fascist apprenticeships locally before widening the fight to Spain. Edinburgh councillor Tom Murray pioneered some effective use of bureaucracy, for example in arguing that the Edinburgh Parks Committee should turn down on the grounds of noise pollution a BUF request to use a loudspeaker for their rally at the Meadows in September 1937. The Committee duly obliged, and Mosley et al. abandoned the meeting. Usually, action against the BUF was far more direct, as in Aberdeen. Bill Cranston, an unemployed chimney sweep from Leith, recalled being involved in numerous street scrapes with fascists, drawing direct parallels between the struggles in Scotland and those in Spain:

Something I didn't like at all were the Blackshirts, the British fascists led by Sir Oswald Mosley. Before we volunteered to go to Spain to help the Spanish republic defend itself against Franco, we used to read a lot about the treatment that the Jews were getting in London at the hands of Mosley's fascists.

George Watters[1], a volunteer from Prestonpans, intervened directly with Mosley as he spoke at the Usher Hall, Edinburgh on 15 May 1936:

I had a front seat and my job was to get up and create a disturbance right away by challenging Sir Oswald Mosley, which I did. At that particular time I had a loud voice, and Mosley wasn't being heard. I was being warned by William Joyce, Lord Haw Haw, what would happen to me unless I was quiet. There was a rush and I got a bit of a knocking about and taken up to the High Street. When I was in the High Street I was accused by one of the fascists of having kicked him on the eye. His eye was split right across. So I just said at the time: 'I wish to Christ it had been me, then at least I would have felt some satisfaction!'

Watters escaped with a fine of five pounds and his determination to continue the fight, whether in Midlothian or Madrid, intact. Also present at the Usher Hall was Donald Renton, another who later served in Spain. During Mosley's speech, Renton, a future Edinburgh councillor, leant over the balcony and gave a stirring rendition of the '*Internationale*', before being forcibly ejected from the building.

Opposition to fascism did not always take the form of organised political demonstration or counter-demonstration. For Steve Fullarton, challenging fascism was a visceral, personal reaction rooted in his sense of humanity. This was pivotal in persuading him to take up in Spain the fight he had waged in his native Shettleston:

Fascism was a terrible thing. And what it was doing to everybody; trade unionists and politicians who were not Nazis. Things like that. And of course it was the bombing, the bombing of civilians that really got on my nerves. I would go to the cinema and see that on the newsreel, see the women running with the bairns in their hands, eyes turned skywards for the planes, to see if they were coming. That was absolutely disgraceful in the twentieth century but it happened, I know it happened. And eventually that's what drove me to offering to join the International Brigades. It was a straightforward thing to say I'd like to join them. All I could do was offer my services and hope it would be worthwhile.

This sense of moral crusade against fascism was apparent in letters sent home once Scotsmen had arrived in Spain. As Glaswegian Alec Park wrote on 27 January 1938:

You of course understand my reasons for coming here, my appreciation of the dangers of fascism, my bitter hatred of fascism and my great desire to have a go where the fight is hottest.

Whether motivated by political conviction or a heartfelt sense of right and wrong, Scots were resolutely moved to fight fascism at home and willing to export that fight abroad. This was underpinned by the notion that if it were not laid to rest in Spain, fascism would come to Britain in the shape of a second world war and subsequent invasion. Prevention of that wider conflict was at the forefront of volunteers' minds, as Tom Murray wrote home:

If only the people of Britain could fully understand the utter brutality of fascism with its bombings of innocent people, they would rise in their wrath and come to the aid of the gallant Spanish people. If our people do not do this now, they cannot escape the necessity of doing much more later to save their own doorstep, and under much more difficult circumstances. On my first night here I was roused from bed by an air-raid alarm and had to spend a shivering time in a trench. I would hate to find that through indifference now my fellow-citizens of Edinburgh and Scotland were to find themselves in such close proximity to the stark realities of war.

In April 1937, Sydney Quinn, of Glasgow, wrote an emotional letter home to his son emphasising the same point:

I am writing this on the eve of going into action against fascism. Whenever I see the thousands of Spanish children streaming along the road away from the fascists, my thoughts revert back home, and I can see you and your brothers in the same circumstances if we don't smash the fascist monsters here.

Contemporary press coverage of events in Spain may also have helped persuade Scots to volunteer. The *News Chronicle*, *Daily Mirror* and *Daily Worker* all outwardly supported the Spanish republic, though it was the latter of those three that offered the most vehement support. The *Worker* was no fringe newspaper, and doubled its British sales over the period of the Spanish war from 100,000 in 1936 to 200,000 in 1939. As credible historical documentation, however, much of its editorial content should be treated questioningly; the paper was unwaveringly Stalinist in this era, for instance greeting the USSR's 1936 constitution with the headline: 'Stalin Opens New World Era – One-sixth of Earth Rejoices in New Charter of Freedom'. Yet its impact in crusading for the Spanish republic is beyond doubt, spearheading as it did countless campaigns of financial support and offering steadfast backing to the International Brigades.

The *Worker* remained optimistic of imminent republican victory until the last days of the war, which can't have gone unnoticed by would-be volunteers weighing up the chances of participating in a quick victory in Spain. More than anything, though, it was the images printed in the communist newspaper that provoked people into action. Just as Steve Fullarton had been disgusted at the movie reels he had witnessed of bombing raids on Madrid, so readers were outraged to see, from November 1936 onwards, graphic images of slaughtered Spaniards.

However, of far greater motivation than newsprint for joining the fight in Spain was the perceived failure of government, Labour Party and trade union policies towards the Spanish republic. The National Governments of Stanley Baldwin and Neville Chamberlain were deeply committed to a policy of neutrality. On 4 August 1936 the British and French governments signed a Non-Intervention Treaty making it illegal for the legitimately elected Spanish republican government and General Franco's nationalists to purchase arms for self-defence. Additionally, the agreement prohibited signatories from sending troops to Spain. The pact was formalised on 9 September with the establishment of a 27 countries strong Non-Intervention Committee. The policy stood throughout the civil war, despite the evident flood of arms and troops supplied to the nationalist side in Spain by Germany and Italy. This myopia when it came to foreign assistance for Franco's side led many of those who joined the International Brigades to believe that the British establishment were in surreptitious support of the military rebellion. Indeed, these misgivings were not without grounds: the British Ambassador to Spain, Henry Chilton, stated in 1937 that 'I am awaiting the time when they shall finally send enough Germans to finish the war.'

When the London government realised that the Non-Intervention Agreement was failing to deter British volunteers from travelling to Spain to fight, it invoked the 1870 Foreign Enlistment Act, from January 1937. This made it illegal for British nationals to participate in Spain's war, though in reality the Act proved impossible to enforce and its adoption was more of a symbolic gesture aimed at underlining the government's policy of non-intervention.

The government's determination to remain officially neutral had the ironic effect of becoming a recruiting sergeant for volunteers: if the elected representatives of the country were to do nothing about Franco's *coup d'état*, then the burden would have to fall on individuals. George Murray, the International Brigader brother of Tom and Annie, who served in Spain as a nurse (see Chapter 7), displayed his contempt for governmental protection of Franco in a letter sent home from the front line:

The very thought of [Anthony] Eden and company makes my blood boil.

'Franco should be granted rights' – 'rights' for the murder of hundreds of thousands of children, women and men. No more reactionary, hateful and deceitful gang of crooks ever disgraced Britain.

Edinburgh's John Gollan, a future leader of the Communist Party of Great Britain (CPGB) who visited Spain twice though didn't fight, summed up the feelings of many volunteers to Spain when he claimed that the Non-Intervention Committee was 'a screen behind which Hitler's and Mussolini's invasion has been carried out'. Interestingly, the policy of non-intervention had the consistent support of both the *Glasgow Herald* and *The Scotsman*, the latter printing an editorial on 22 February 1937 that asserted 'the future government of Spain is a question which should be settled by Spain alone'.

Against this backdrop of institutional hostility to aiding the Spanish republic, many of its supporters in Scotland looked to the Scottish Labour Party for guidance. However, at a joint conference between the national Labour Party and Trade Union Congress (TUC) on 28 August 1936, a policy of neutrality on Spain was declared. This was reaffirmed at a further conference in Edinburgh in October 1936, when, despite significant support for intervention in Spain among union members, the policy of neutrality received 1,836,000 votes for and only 590,000 against. Yet by the end of that month, both the Labour Party and the TUC had declared against non-intervention, and advocated the republic's right to buy arms. These, though, were constitutional moves, and very little practical assistance was offered in campaigning against Franco.

At the top of the Scottish Labour Party, support for the Spanish republic appeared lukewarm and debate on Spain at the Scottish Council of the Labour Party's 1937 conference was banned. Scottish Labour's Secretary, Arthur Woodburn, was opposed to any unified action on Spain, much to the chagrin of the CPGB in its efforts to build a Unity Campaign. In the newspaper *Forward*, the vehicle of the Scottish Labour left, he wrote that 'Peace Councils, Anti-Fascist Committees and Anti-War Organisations are useless', and frequently criticised CPGB activity. As George Murray concluded in a letter home, action on Spain from the Labour leadership was barely existent:

The Labour Party has been petrified for so long that it is next to impossible to make it move now. Spain has already paid heavily and tragically for that inertia.

On the subject of British non-intervention and Labour Party inaction, William McDade, of Dundee, wrote from the Jarama front with a similar, if more desperate message:

If Britain is going to withdraw her ships and leave the coast to German and Italian warships to bombard defenceless towns filled with women and children, and say it is to save Christianity, then Britain is openly helping Franco. Our comrades at home must raise hell and get the workers on the move over the question: what is Labour doing about it?

If Scottish supporters of the Spanish republic felt betrayed and isolated by the government and the Labour Party, it was with good reason. They fared little better in looking to the Scottish Trade Union Congress (STUC) for dynamic leadership or support. As with the Britain-wide TUC, the STUC only belatedly condemned non-intervention and endorsed the republic; even then, it was slow in offering actual aid to the cause.

Within the STUC, there was something of a chasm between a leadership cool on support for the Spanish republic and a membership keen to do what they could, from fundraising to fighting. This schism was largely a consequence of splits within the Scottish left caused by Labour's 1931 election defeat and the disaffiliation of the ILP a year later, events which also influenced the atmosphere of discordance between the Labour Party and its own members on Spain.

The STUC vigorously resisted affiliation with Aid Committees and similar organisations until 1939, and it was left to members to form their own 'unofficial' alliances, such as Glasgow and Edinburgh Trade Councils' Arms and Ammunition for Spain group, formed in February 1938. Individual trade union branches gave solid backing to the republic for the duration of the war in Spain, whether through the passing of supporting motions, direct fundraising, or leaning on their local Trades Councils to stage demonstrations.

However, the STUC's failure to organise a co-ordinated campaign of support for the republic until it was too late meant that the Scottish trade union movement was denied the influence it could have had, and Scots longing to aid republican Spain would have to take the initiative for themselves.

For some Scottish volunteers, the chance to help preserve reforms enacted by the Spanish republican government acted as a further, if less weighty, motivation for travelling, as George Watters confirmed:

We were afraid of the situation developing, of what was likely to happen to the Spanish Government, which at that particular time was carrying through some very good measures so far as the ordinary people were concerned: the eight-hour day, compulsory education for all children, a guaranteed wage and a number of other features that were considered a great advance.

In somewhat grandiose terms, Tom Murray described his work in Spain as a revolutionary experience, writing home to his wife in April 1938:

> We are comrades in a great campaign, co-workers in a magnificent
> enterprise and a determined team of builders in the work for the Socialist
> Commonwealth.

While this fits in with *The Scotsman*'s February 1937 description of
volunteers as being 'anxious to fight for the communist cause embodied in
the International Brigade', sentiments such as these often took a back seat to
the reality of fighting the war once active service commenced. Though George
Drever, an erudite Brigader from Leith, saw elements of building socialism
in Spain and was willing to stay around for the journey post-civil war, even
he railed against groups such as the Partido Obrero de Unificacíon Marxista,
or POUM (see Chapter 11), who wanted to instigate a revolution while
simultaneously fighting Franco's forces, rather than concentrating on winning
the war first. Brigader Garry McCartney, a blacksmith from Dennistoun who
had participated in the 1926 General Strike, went further in an interview with
the *Glasgow Evening Times*:

> We weren't fighting for communism, we just wanted to beat the fascists.
> The Germans and Italians could have been stopped in their tracks in
> Spain if Britain and France had just let us get on with it.

Having spent a year in a Gestapo-run concentration camp replete with gas
chambers, McCartney knew the evils of fascism more than most by the time
he had finished in Spain. Donald Renton supported his view of why Scots
volunteered, remarking 'the struggle in Spain was not a struggle to establish
communism, but a struggle to preserve democracy against the fascist threat.'[2]

For a small number of volunteers, motivations for signing up to fight in
Spain appear less wholesome. George Watters admitted that early on in the
war, prior to the tightening of discipline within the ranks of the International
Brigades, some had 'got away with going in, getting a certain amount of money
and never being seen again'. 'Naturally', he admitted, 'you had the adventurer
and the boy that was trying to get something.' John Dunlop, a learned Glasgow
recruit, suspected one man he knew in Spain had run away from Scotland
to escape a woman he'd 'bairned', though that particular Brigader became
zealously committed to the cause and returned home solidly politicised.

Jimmy Maley claimed that both Charlie 'Cheeky' McCaig of the notorious
Garngad Cheeky Forty gang and members of the Union Jack Rangers
Supporters Club set out for Spain, though he was unsure as to whether the
men had made it out of Britain. Their motives can only be speculated upon;

perhaps Cheeky McCaig was escaping gangland trouble at home and anti-Catholicism may have played a part in the case of the Union Jack group.

The pro-neutrality *Scotsman* ran a story on 30 October 1937 undermining the stimuli of two Scottish volunteers and the British Battalion (the division of the republican army Scottish volunteers joined from January 1937) as a whole. The newspaper reported having spoken to a Scots duo in Spain awaiting repatriation by the 'long-suffering British Government'. One of the two, a trained pilot, was in his second spell in Spain after an initial period in which he had 'spent most of his flying time... hiding in clouds to avoid combat with the enemy'. This time, ran the story, he hadn't even got that far, as the Spanish republican air service had now filled their quota of airmen with natives.

The second man, formerly a machine-gunner with the Territorial Army, had expected to be given a high rank on arrival in Spain but was instructed to join the Brigades as an infantry private. Disgruntled at this but still desirous of an adventure, the men had considered joining the French Foreign Legion before resolving instead to request repatriation from the British Consulate. Both, implied *The Scotsman*, had gone to Spain only to escape the boredom of their domestic lives; it described the pilot volunteer as 'just an irresponsible youngster'. Neither man was named in the story and no quotations offered. The piece ended with the telling and short-sighted description of the British Battalion as 'a curious episode in the history of the British people'.

Despite *The Scotsman*'s attempts to portray volunteers as gullible and disparate adventure-seekers, they were, in fact, generally united by pure motivations, and overwhelmingly united by their social backgrounds. John Dunlop said of his compatriot Brigaders, 'I only knew one middle-class type, and that was me.' Those who fought mainly came from a range of working-class jobs; there were coal miners, painters, printers, engineers, builders and even a lemonade salesman. There were, too, a considerable number of unemployed labourers in Spain, and a small cluster of middle-class students, obviously unknown to Dunlop.

Most Scots volunteers came from urban and industrial areas, chiefly Aberdeen, Dundee, Edinburgh, Fife, Glasgow and Lanarkshire. Glasgow, and specifically the Maryhill, Springburn and Bridgeton (despite the best efforts of the Billy Boys) areas, provided up to one half of all Scottish volunteers.

Politically, around 60 per cent were in the CPGB, while a fifth of volunteers spread their allegiances between the Labour Party and the ILP. A further fifth had no formal allegiance or membership. Commitment to the party political cause varied between Brigaders: some, like Bob Cooney and Peter Kerrigan, were significant Communist Party figures, while others, like Steve Fullarton and Willie Gauntlet, only joined the Party once in Spain and drifted away over time. A number were members of two parties at once; Tom Murray, as a councillor, admitted to being 'above board Labour and clandestine Communist'.

Despite the significant influence of the Communist Party on the International Brigades and their members, until late on in the Spanish Civil War there was no organised recruitment process in Scotland, with would-be volunteers making their own way to Spain until mid-1937. Thereafter, such journeys were facilitated by the strategic and financial help of the Scottish District Committee of the Communist Party, based at 83 Ingram Street, Glasgow.

There were, however, Party men throughout Scotland who would sound out possible volunteers and inform them about life on the front line in Spain, as well as vetting them for suitability. George Murray recalled being 'more or less recruited' by Jack Morrison, an influential member of the Spanish Aid Committee[3]. Jock MacDonald, a poacher from Cambuslang and thus adroit with a gun, was interviewed by CPGB man Geordie Middleton, who was slightly put off when he learnt that MacDonald had 18 children. With dependents' pay at five shillings per child, Middleton is said to have replied to the volunteer: 'We could get a general for that, never mind a poacher!'

By spring 1938, with heavy defeats meaning losses in men and dwindling morale, Battalion representatives began to pursue volunteers in Scotland, with local Communist Party branches working to centrally-defined recruitment targets. Recruitment had slowed as it became clear that this was to be a drawn-out war with no fixed term of maximum service. Coatbridge volunteer Alec Donaldson referred, albeit comically, to the slow drip of recruits later in the conflict when writing back to Scotland in April 1938:

Aberdeen seems to be sending a good type of comrade – so does Scotland generally – but the quantity isn't enough. How about running a 'Cruise Down the Clyde' for males only, and then ship them here instead?

Whatever the process of recruitment, with contact made and approval granted, volunteers were ready to set out for Spain, most never having left their home country before.

CHAPTER 2

Bonny Voyage:
Leaving Scotland, Arriving in Spain

I ought to get a chance to mow down one or two
fascist bastards before very long
John Miller, Alexandria

My Dear Tom
Just a note before you leave Britain to tell you how sad but proud I feel
at the thought of how much you, George and Annie are prepared to
sacrifice for the great ideals we all hold for the betterment and happiness
of humanity. I just can't tell you how much we shall miss you and dread
the thought of the awful dangers you will face; but through all the
anxiety and sadness, we will know that you had the supreme satisfaction
that you had done the very utmost you could. I can only wish you all the
luck possible and look forward to the proud day when you will come
back to us all.
Much love, your affectionate sister, Lily xxx

THE LEAVING OF Scotland for Spain usually meant a gathering of volunteers in Glasgow for the onward journey to London. The size of party they travelled in varied; Tommy Bloomfield recalled registering in a group of 150, while Steve Fullarton journeyed with only five others, three of whom (Jimmy Reid, Willie Gauntlet and Willie Dougan) were close neighbours of his in Shettleston.

The work of processing new recruits fell to Isa Alexander at the Ingram Street headquarters. From Glasgow, volunteers would be conveyed to London via train or bus, often being sent off by cheering crowds. Jimmy Maley recalled the sense of adventure boarding the bus engendered: 'It was like a Celtic supporters' outing. I recognised some of them who'd gone to school with me.'[4] Maley travelled in the same party of 150 as Bloomfield, three buses leaving George Square in December 1936, their passengers paying £5 8s. (£5.40) each for the privilege of riding towards war.

Not all volunteers were surrounded by the same buoyant atmosphere as they departed. John Dunlop had to elude the attentions of his father and uncle who, desperate for him not to give up his promising career as an accountant to go to Spain, attempted to head their young relative off at the railway station.

Aberdonian Archie Dewar (front left) poses with British and Spanish comrades. On arrival in Spain, Scottish volunteers were often struck by the sense of solidarity that existed between the different nationalities of the International Brigades.

The determined Dunlop, though, boarded the 5pm train rather than the 6pm as anticipated, and arrived in London in time to take part in the May Day Rally of 1937.

Once in London, volunteers were divided into groups and instructed to wait, usually in Euston Station, while designated group leaders journeyed to Communist Party buildings to gather money for train fares. Having collected these funds, weekend return tickets to Paris were purchased for the key reason that travel on these tourist trains did not require passengers to show a passport – very few of those travelling to Spain from Scotland had ever required or been able to afford one. The ticket, Steve Fullarton recalled 70 years on, cost 28s. 6d., and included passage on the Newhaven to Dieppe ferry, and then onward rail travel to Paris.

In Paris, volunteers faced a short wait until the time was right to move on to the French border with Spain. Tom Murray, granted eight months' leave from council duties to serve in Spain, was put in charge of 35 men, including 11 Scots, one of whom was Fullarton, 19 years his junior, for the French leg of the journey. In an April 1938 letter home to his wife Janet, Murray, a leading figure in the Scottish Temperance Movement, put this elevation to leadership down to his sobriety:

> It was amusing to be strongly urged by the comrade in charge in Paris to rigorously exclude drink from my mind until I got to Spain. He was very strong on the point and I think the fact I announced myself a tee-totaller was the principle factor in the decision to make me a group leader.

This was certainly modest; in truth, Murray excelled in Spain and showed himself to be a born leader of men, as was indicated in the decision to make him a Political Commissar with the machine-gun company of the British Battalion. He later described the scene as those 35 men waited in a dormitory in Béziers, a French border town, ahead of their crossing into Spain:

> My comrades are all determined opponents of fascism and have spent most of this forenoon in heated political discussions. They are mostly people who have never been out of their native land before.

In addition to Scots, this group included Austrians, Czechoslovakians, Dutchmen, Germans and Italians, all energised by a heady mix of excitement, nervousness and political conviction. Volunteer John Ross, whose father had fallen at the Somme, enjoyed the forging of a similar comradeship upon his arrival in France several months earlier:

In Paris, we stayed one night, eating our meals at a co-operative restaurant filled with people of every possible nationality, all united by a common purpose, based on international ideology: a most stimulating experience, I found.

Steve Fullarton's morale was boosted in a very personal way; between leaving Glasgow and arriving in Paris, he managed to age from 18 years old to 22, which was 'not bad, especially at that age, where one year makes a difference.' As he explained:

I told the Communist Party organiser in Shettleston where I lived that I wanted to go and join the International Brigades, and he told me before we went to the Party office in Glasgow: 'You'd better say you're 19.' He went to the office and he came out and said: 'You can go, but you've to say you're 20.' And when we got to London and [Chris] Smith got back with the money from the Party office he says: 'Oh, you have got to be 21.' Then in the medical examination in Paris, the doctor said 'You have to be 22 to join, so by now I just says, 'I *am* 22.'

In the medical examination Fullarton referred to, he had initially been rejected for being 'flat-footed', but argued his corner until he was permitted to join the Brigades. Formal medical and political screening of volunteers in Paris was carried out only from early 1938. Prior to that date, there had been instances of budding one-armed soldiers being admitted in to Spain, and an ethos that any volunteers with dubious personal or political credentials could be easily detected without formal scrutiny, as John Dunlop recalled:

In my experience, there was no screening of volunteers neither in Paris nor on the way through France, nor in Spain itself: there was hardly any need for it, as any elements that might be considered 'disruptive' stood out like sore thumbs and became obvious candidates for surveillance.

After Paris, the new Brigaders moved on through France towards the Pyrenees, usually on board the 'red train', to gather in Perpignan and nearby towns such as Cerbère and Béziers for transportation by bus to crossing points. While waiting in Perpignan on the night they were to leave for their passage into Spain, John Dunlop enjoyed a good meal and some old-fashioned Dutch courage in a local café, quaffing, as he wrote in *Blue Blanket* magazine 'a flagon of wine, sour red stuff. It was our Stirrup Cup and made us feel fit for anything.'[5]

Passport checks by local police were often carried out on the buses trans-

Bill Cranston (bottom left) with English and Greek comrades, grateful to have eluded the 'fascists in Perpignan' and arrived in Spain.

porting volunteers towards the French–Spanish border (France, after all, was a signatory of the Non-Intervention Agreement).

The *Gendarmes* seemed generally sympathetic to the cause of those travelling, and often bent the rules to admit passengers without passports through, as George Watters stated:

From Perpignan there were buses, and they [the police] came on and checked you had a passport to go on to Spain. One fellow in the bus had a passport. Whenever they came in he showed his passport and they were quite satisfied. They were obviously all sympathetic and knew what was happening. We all went through quite easily.

Donald Renton, in charge of Watters' group, also remarked upon this:

We crossed the frontier in relative comfort, and the guards in broad measure appeared to indicate to us a considerable sympathy for the aims that we were seeking to achieve in terms of support for the Spanish republic.[6]

From now until the men were safely in Spain, silence and stealth were vital in order to avoid the attentions of any French officials actually obeying the Non-Intervention Agreement, and local fascists liable to 'shop' those attempting to fight Franco's forces. As Bill Cranston observed, 'we were told to speak among ourselves, and only in whispers. It seems there were a lot of fascists in Perpignan.' The quiet went on as the volunteers boarded the large, canvas-hooded charabancs which were to transport them to the foot of the Pyrenees, each man ducking to avoid detection when other vehicles passed. John Dunlop recalled in *Blue Blanket* that the silence was finally broken by defiant laughter as the charabancs raced towards their drop-off points:

Exhilaration frothed in our veins. We laughed at the laws and interna-

tional agreements made to forbid us in our mission, at the venal politicians who had made them and at the police and military who were
charged with the duty of preventing us. A feeling of triumph seemed to
trumpet all over us.

Amidst sweeping searchlights, the Brigaders disembarked and were told
to follow practised guides on their long and tortuous night time treks over
the Pyrenees in what Steve Fullarton called 'a game of follow the leader'.
Conditions were not for the fainthearted: the men, Dunlop wrote, hauled
their way up 'by hand, through pine trees whose roots clawed through their
bed of soft needles into the jutting rocks below.' The trekkers faced the dual
perils of treacherous terrain and patrol guards. Their relief at making it over
the border into Spain was immense.

The comradeship built up in these testing conditions was evident in the
bonhomie that usually accompanied volunteers' entries into Spain. Dunlop
described in stirring terms his arrival at a mountainside cookhouse, where he
found coffee, bread and comrades from across the world awaiting him and his
travel partners. After mutual back-slapping, recollected Dunlop:

The singing started, such singing as I had never heard the like of, each
nation singing its own workers' song of protest till the building became
filled with a volume of sound that gradually swelled into one glorious
chorale – The '*Internationale*' – sung together in a dozen different
tongues. Words cannot express the exaltation that surged in our hearts.
This was the greatest moment of our lives.

The hike into Spain over the Pyrenees took seven or eight hours. The
volunteers' real journey had only just begun.

While the route was well-trodden and generally successful for Scottish
volunteers, journeys did not always run smoothly. Glaswegians Andrew Winter
and William Duncan were arrested along with nine others attempting to make
a routine night crossing of the Pyrenees. From their cell, the prisoners issued
a joint statement that declared, 'I have come direct from my country with the
intention of going to Spain and helping my republican comrades.' Winter did
eventually make it into Spain, sadly perishing in battle near Brunete.

On arrival in France, Dundonian Frank McCusker, a participant in the
1936 NUWM march to London, was deported as a vagrant, yet still contrived
to make it over the Pyrenees three days later. Another Dundonian, Tom Clarke,
faced an altogether more slapstick form of adversity. On departing his home
city, he was given a packet of cigarettes containing a secret message to be

Republican soldiers set off for the front line in a buoyant mood.
The slogan daubed on the side of their carriage reads: 'O brothers, swear on these words:
it is better to die than to allow tyrants'.

handed over to a Communist Party contact in Paris. Clarke, though, suffered an unfortunate craving on his journey to France and contrived to smoke the one cigarette in the pack containing the message.

A number of resolute Scots made it to Spain completely under their own steam. Hugh MacKay, from Perth, deserted the French Foreign Legion in 1934, and eventually found his way to Spain to fight on the government side. Imprisoned by republican authorities as a spy for the very act of managing to make his own way into Spain, he was eventually freed and served in the British Battalion at the Ebro and Gandesa. Falkirk lad Sam Hannah was possibly the youngest Scot to travel to Spain, having been born in 1920. On hearing of the Spanish Civil War, he joined the ss *Aitkenside*, then docked at Grangemouth, and sailed, via France, to Bilbao. At 16, he was deemed too young to fight, and so became a runner with the American Abraham Lincoln Brigade, serving at Madrid, Jarama and Ebro.

Following the outbreak of civil war, the very first Scottish arrivals in Spain were tooled with bagpipes rather than rifles. Four pipers were selected to play at the week-long Peoples' Olympiad in Barcelona from 19 July 1936, and while there headed a march of workers from the Catalan city to Zaragoza. They returned at the end of the games, though the *Daily Worker* claimed the pipers had expressed a desire to fight for the republic. That wish unfulfilled, there was a trickle of Scottish volunteers from August onwards, until larger numbers began to arrive from December.

British volunteers would usually arrive at Figueras in the Spanish north, something of a holding base, before being transferred to the International Brigade headquarters at Albacete, and then the nearby village of Madrigueras for training (after the summer of 1937, instruction took place at Tarazona de la Mancha). On reporting for duty, they were issued with khaki uniforms featuring Balmoral-style caps, strong boots and a food-cum-shaving bowl.

The little-travelled volunteers were often astounded by the eclecticism of their new international comrades. Tom Murray expressed this view in a letter dated 10 April 1938:

> What an inspiration it is to find oneself among fine fellows from practically every country in Europe, America and Canada – including Germans and Italians, some of the latter two having escaped from fascist hands. I wish that all of you in Britain could just experience the emotions and thrilling sensations which my experience has given me.

Upon his own arrival, Donald Renton was similarly enthralled by the sight of female participants defending the republic:

> For the first time we saw the militiawomen, comrades who like ourselves were either going to have or had already had first hand experience in battle conditions against the fascist enemy. These were wonderful comrades, people who had, so far as I was concerned at least, a very very powerful, inspirational effect.[7]

One month to six weeks of basic military training would commence for recent recruits soon after their arrival. For much of the war, describing the training as 'basic' appears generous at best. George Murray was probably closest when he described it as 'more or less useless'.[8]

Steve Fullarton was alarmed to find that, due to a chronic lack of equipment, shooting practice was undertaken with mock-up wooden rifles. Where it did exist, much of the weaponry used in training and combat dated from the first quarter of the 20th century and earlier; battered old Lewis and Chauchat guns were deployed, despite being more suited to the scrapheap than the battlefield. Renton commented:

What little training we were getting was training based on weapons that were completely obsolete. They were as liable to explode in your face if they were actually used, and most of them were donkeys' years old and of no use what so ever in terms of actual battle conditions.[9]

This exacerbated the problems caused by the inexperience of volunteers. William Jackson, a 41-year-old Glaswegian who had fought in World War One, estimated that 80 per cent of arrivals at the training camp where he was an instructor had never seen a rifle before. Jackson was assiduous in his task nonetheless, Jimmy Maley remarking that: 'Willy took his job seriously, helping to instil confidence in many of the younger men including me.'

In the absence of suitable firearms, an emphasis was placed on marching, as Renton verified:

I got six weeks training at Madrigueras. This began with essential weapons training, this being the result of Tom Wintringham's influence. He was a most effective instructor, who believed the importance of co-ordinated foot drill would be clear to us once we could handle our weapons.

As the Soviet Union began to send aid to the republican side, the equipment shortage did lessen somewhat. Jimmy Maley commented on the sudden improvements prompted by the arrival of Soviet arms:

It was chaotic, and it seemed to take a long time. We sat around for three or four weeks; there was no training, until all of a sudden the stuff had arrived.[10]

The arrival of Soviet help was welcome and, for some, awe-inspiring. Jimmy Moir, a 19-year-old who was to die brutally at Brunete, wrote back from behind the lines in June 1937:

For the first time today I saw a Russian aeroplane in flight. It seemed to be of advanced design and had two engines which propelled it at great speed. Chaps at the front say that our bombers are faster than the enemy fighters.

John Dunlop too talked of the positive impact Soviet Chatos aeroplanes had, and the 'marvellous' anti-tank guns provided by Moscow. Donald Renton went further:

In Madrigueras, for the first time we saw Russian rifles and I'll never forget that day because at that particular time I worshipped the Soviet Union. When one finally had a rifle on which one could depend to do a specific job, in terms of killing fascists and not killing yourself, and with a hammer and sickle emblazed on it, then one felt a real thrill of pride.[11]

This undoubtedly made training more useful as time progressed, though quality equipment was always in short supply, and as such pre-fighting instruction remained basic; long periods of marching, shooting (or 'shooting'), and learning how to take cover were of some value, but far from realistic preparation for the brutality of battle.

CHAPTER 3

Early Action:
Brunete and Jarama

It is a tragedy that we had to lose so many fine comrades. That of course is war which, as we have often said before, is pure hell.

George Murray, Glasgow

THE FIRST SCOTS to arrive in Spain intent on fighting rather than piping were lucky if they received *any* training, 'useless' or otherwise. Early participants fought as part of militia groups such as the English-speaking Tom Mann Centuria, though even that troop was manned primarily by French and German volunteers. Jock Cunningham, an early volunteer from Coatbridge who would attain legendary status during the conflict, joined the Commune de Paris Battalion, a part of the XIth International Brigade charged with defending the north-west of Madrid during an early nationalist offensive.

The foreign militias were fairly rag-tag, ill-equipped groups, yet they fought heroically and tenaciously. John Gollan described them as an 'army in overalls', though he noted that of those applying to be in the militias, Spanish or otherwise, virtually none had any previous military experience to speak of. Inevitably, they suffered heavy losses, including those of Scottish recruits such as Martin Messer, a 24-year-old hotel worker from Glasgow who had arrived in London on a hunger march and elected to continue onwards to Spain. Messer was killed in a battle with German troops in the University City area to the northwest of Madrid in December 1936, as the nationalists advanced, ultimately unsuccessfully, on that sector of the capital. Glaswegian Phil Gillan, fighting next to Messer, conveyed the intensity of the assault:

> In spite of my 'terror' training, I was just plain scared – and I'm not ashamed to admit it – the zip, zip got louder and then suddenly I knew that the air was just thick with machine-gun bullets. Did I duck? You bet I did.[12]

Gillan somehow survived that particular bombardment, though only just, as George Murray reported:

He has been shot through the neck and had a miraculous escape from death. The bullet affected a nerve in one of his arms which is now partly out of action, but there is chance more or less of a complete recovery.

Gillan was invalided home, leaving behind the horrific Madrid conditions that Roddy MacFarquhar of the Scottish Ambulance Unit (see Chapter 6), was met with on his arrival there in January 1937:

I'll never forget those first few days – it was my first experience of war – and one image that has always stuck in my mind is of a Spanish woman running with her three children for shelter. Suddenly they were caught in a burst of shrapnel. I ran to help them, but one of the children had taken it in the belly and I could see she wasn't going to live.

Other early Scottish involvement in battle occurred at Lopera, a town deep in the south of Spain. Around 150 British volunteers had been formed into a company (named the Saklatvalas, after the Indian-born British communist politician of the same name) of the French Battalion and instructed to capture the nationalist-held town on Christmas Eve 1936.

The Saklatvalas, including in their ranks Jock Cunningham and Dundonians James Cockburn and Ken Stalker, were soon repelled and forced to retreat.

However, the formal unification of British troops in one company at Lopera had proven that militarily the formation of a larger group along the same lines was a feasible option, and in January 1937 the new British Battalion was created, becoming part of the xvth (English-speaking) International Brigade.

They were soon to be propelled into intense action.

Glaswegian Tommy Flynn, killed at Cordoba while fighting as part of the German section of the Chapayev Battalion of the XIIIth International Brigade. Flynn also took part in the assault on Lopera, an action which hastened the establishment of a British Battalion.

At the Jarama valley, straddled around the river of the same name to the south-east of Madrid, the newly-formed British Battalion were primed for their pivotal defensive duties as part of the xvth International Brigade. For those early members of the Battalion now waiting nervously to defend the Madrid to Valencia road as the nationalists advanced upon the capital, the excitement of the journey to Spain was over, the warm-ups completed, and bloody battle imminent.

The Battalion were to be lead by Scotsman Wilfred McCartney, an author and former British Army soldier fresh from a decade in Parkhurst prison, having been found guilty of spying for the Soviet Union. Yet McCartney was never to see battle. On the night of 5 February 1937, as McCartney and Peter Kerrigan exchanged pistols ahead of the former's impending parole trip to Britain, one of the guns went off, injuring McCartney. What happened did not pass without controversy; some later alleged that the event was no accident, and that certain factions within the CPGB had wanted McCartney out of the way. What is certain is that Kerrigan expressed great remorse at what had occurred, and even asked to be repatriated with McCartney, writing to CPGB headquarters on 10 February:

> I asked to be sent home with him. The accident was the result of a stupid mistake for which I was responsible and it was just chance that the consequences were not a great deal more serious.

With McCartney returned to Britain due to his injuries, Tom Wintringham, an Englishman, took command of the Battalion. Under Wintringham, Jock Cunningham was promoted to Commander of the Battalion's No. 1 Company (there were four companies in all, three regular and one, No. 2 Company, machine-gunner).

The Glaswegian Kerrigan, domestically the CPGB's representative to the Comintern and in Spain the commissar for English-speaking International Brigaders at Albacete, wrote to Harry Pollitt, CPGB leader, as the 500-plus strong Battalion left their training base at Madrigueras on 9 February bound for Jarama. Kerrigan displayed optimism and pride, but also an awareness that many would perish in the battle to come:

> The boys looked splendid today when we left them. They are keen and I think very efficient. They know what is expected of them and will do their best to carry out the job. I felt bloody rotten when I shook hands with Springie and George and dozens of others. After all I know dozens of them personally. I came out with them, and I've seen the Battalion shape itself from the beginning. I know all the arguments about this sort

of reaction (I've listened to them out here at headquarters) but it is not possible to feel otherwise. You shake hands with lads and know that for some it's the last time you'll do it. What they don't visualise clearly is the really historic part they are playing. They are too close to it all to see that history is being made here, and that this present generation and those that follow will be filled with a great pride at the way these lads have responded. After all it is no little thing to hold back international fascism and help also to save the peace of the world for a little longer.

Even for such makers of history, preparations for the battle were worryingly last minute, as Tommy Bloomfield testified:

The xvth Brigade arrived in Chinchon late on 10 February 1937. We of No. 2 Company were given that night to learn how to work with the Russian water-cooled Maxim. We were on our way to the front.

Though the machine-gunners did remarkably attain some cohesion, such ill-preparedness resulted, perhaps inevitably, in further mistakes and early slaughter for the British Battalion, as Bloomfield related:

No. 1 Company attacked a hill in front and slightly left of our machine-gun company which we named Suicide Hill. They took an awful beating and had to retreat. Through a mix-up we got the wrong ammo for our guns. The battle raged on through the 12th [February] into the 13th. We had sorted our problems during the night. In the morning the fascists tried to attack with a battalion of Moorish cavalry which were completely slaughtered by our eight machine-guns. With that they threw everything that they had at our position. They shelled, bombed, left overhead shrapnel on us. Unknown to us No. 4 Company had retired on our right flank which meant that we could not control the dead ground in front of our position which No. 4 Company had. This allowed the fascists to infiltrate this ground and come round our back and cut us off. When we realised what had happened, it was too late. Of our 120 men, three had gone back for ammo, we had 29 survivors, and the rest were killed.

Jimmy Maley, another machine-gunner, described being taken up to position and jumping off the back of a truck, guns firing, straight into battle.

Men started to die right there and then. There were men just dropping around us, people from our own group. There were about 28 of us and we were running on. All of a sudden, it stopped.

Maley's group had fired on until entirely out of ammunition. Much of the machine-gun company was subsequently captured by nationalist forces (see Chapter 4). Maley highlighted the tactical weaknesses of the Battalion as a reason for the isolation of his Company:

> After 200 yards going forward, the retreat was coming back and going down past us and we were going through. There were soldiers running past us and we were going up. And there were soldiers of the British Battalion dropping as we were going up. Without firing a shot they were getting killed.

Yet the British Battalion managed to regroup. Against all the odds, as night fell on 14 February, the Battalion began to stand its ground, eventually pushing back in to the areas it had previously retreated from. By the end of February, they had successfully stemmed the advances of the nationalists, and more than held their own. Because of this, Jarama was seen as something of a victory for the republican side, though losses were heavy. Well over a quarter of the 500 British Battalion men who had gone into battle were killed, and a comparable number wounded. The number of Scots in each group was high. Those wounded became so in the most agonising of circumstances. Tom Clarke, a stretcher-bearer, was shot in the head in an area so delicate that doctors refused to remove the bullet. Instead, and without anaesthetic, a dentist extracted the shell. Around 35 Scottish Brigaders died during the main days of fighting at Jarama. Bob Mason, of Edinburgh, was killed when a burning object fell on top of him. His family wrote a glowing tribute to him, which was published in the *Daily Worker* on 25 March 1937:

> When Bob volunteered to go to Spain, it was not with the object of personal gain or with the spirit of adventure. He had every reason to hate fascism by his knowledge of the brutal and murderous suppression of the working class movement under Hitler and Mussolini. The lives of these comrades who have fallen in the fight will not have been sacrificed in vain, and the Spanish Government will be victorious.

Such sentiments, whether printed in newspapers or contained in private correspondence, were a typical reaction for relatives of those lost in Spain. The family of another of the Jarama fallen, James Rae, wrote to the *Worker*:

> You can tell the comrades that though we felt a pang of sorrow, we have no regrets because we know that he died for the cause that he loved so well, and hoping that we who are left behind will keep the flag flying.

Anti-fascism often ran in families, who supported each other in the shared belief that no death was in vain, no matter the personal pain a parent or sibling might feel.

The death at Jarama of Jock Gilmour, a Prestonpans miner, was described by his friend George Watters:

> Before we were surrounded I advised him to wait on them coming up with the ambulance men that would take him down on stretchers. But he felt that it was needed for men that were more severely wounded than he was. He didn't realise how bad he was and unfortunately he died as a result of his wound. He was pumping blood out.

Emphasising the enormity of loss, Bill Gilmour, another World War One veteran, expressed his horror at the harrowing sight of so many Jarama burial sites:

> My heart throbs at the sight of those graves, and as the memory of those boys comes back to me, with all their gestures, jokes and good humour, their political understanding between one another, I can't help but shed a silent tear. Often I think of them when alone in my dug-out or on guard at night by my machine-gun. If Britain only knew what they owed those dead heroes, they would give them as much room in their sentiments as they give to the Unknown Soldiers of the Great War.

It was in this atmosphere that Possilpark Brigader Alex McDade wrote what was to become the British Battalion's anthem, 'There's a valley in Spain called Jarama'. Its bittersweet first verse encapsulated Battalion mood at that juncture:

> *There's a valley in Spain called Jarama,*
> *That's a place that we all know so well,*
> *For 'tis there that we wasted our manhood,*
> *And most of our old age as well.*

Yet the British Battalion had displayed courage and aptitude of the very highest order at Jarama. That they were able to achieve even a stalemate after the debilitating early losses they suffered was a breathtaking accomplishment. Holding back the nationalists at Jarama created a sense of optimism among the xvth Brigade, especially within the British Battalion after their heroics during the night of 14 February. Jock Cunningham summed up the prevailing feeling in the spring of 1937, pronouncing that 'the tide turned at Jarama.'

A year into the war, discipline had been tightened, and the International Brigades began to share some characteristics with regular armies.

Bolstered by events at Jarama, in the middle of 1937 the British Battalion planned for their first offensive of the war, at Brunete, to the west of Madrid. The aim was to encircle nationalist troops in that area. Jock Cunningham felt that Battalion morale was high and discipline good, reporting to Harry Pollitt on 8 May: 'I am pleased to say that everything is showing marked improvements, discipline is tightening up.'

This mood was echoed among rank and file soldiers. In an early June letter to friends in Blairgowrie, Bill Gilmour wrote that:

In spite of provocations, of Almeria, Guernica, Malaga, in spite of the Non-Intervention Committee, in spite of the many difficulties our government are facing and have faced, we are winning. And my heart is singing that I am privileged to serve so active a government.

Soon after the republican advance began, on 6 July, Gilmour wrote home again, articulating a sense of defiance:

We are still in the front line trenches and still happy and healthy. We fight solely for our principles, and the only reward we seek is the final

The Anti-tank Battery of the XVth Brigade, formed in May 1937 ahead of the offensive at Brunete. Eddie Brown recalled that 'In the Anti-Tank Battery there must have been about ten Scotsmen at least, about half the men'. Those alongside Brown included Bill Cranston, John Dunlop, George Murray and Fraser Crombie, the latter tragically killed at Brunete.

defeat of that fascist monster that machine-guns women and children from the air. If necessary, I will renounce my nationality and become a Spaniard, so that I may be privileged to help attain that end.

This defiance, though, was not enough to prevent the offensive becoming almost immediately bogged down, with enormous losses of Battalion personnel. Gilmour hinted at the tactical nous and cynical brutality of the nationalist forces in the same letter:

Their [the fascists'] retreat was organised and it demonstrated the fact that they had clear military strategists which reminded me of the manoeuvres of the Great War. There was nothing too vile for them to stoop to to save their filthy hides. At Villanueva de Cañada they placed women and children between our guns and theirs so that their withdrawal might be easier.

Also at Villanueva de Cañada, Gilmour received an interesting insight into the influence of religion on the nationalist side. When the Battalion managed to capture nationalist trenches there, inside they found holy emblems and prayer books, and 'a circular written in Spanish reminding the soldiers that they were fighting to save religion from menace by reds'.

Yet Gilmour and comrades did not have long to ponder their finds. The scale of human carnage at Brunete swiftly became clear. When Aberdonian David Anderson escaped hospital for a return to the Brunete front, he discovered that only 24 of the 106-man Company he had left behind remained. The rest were dead or severely wounded.

Heavily involved as at Jarama, many Scots were among the casualties. Fraser Crombie, of the Anti-tank Battery, died a quite horrific death, as Rutherglen volunteer Chris Smith explained:

> We were being shelled and unfortunately one of them caught Kirkcaldy lad Fraser Crombie in the chest. Myself and a guy called Hugh Slater crawled out to get the body. Halfway there Slater told me to cross over, and when we reached the remains I realised that he did it to keep me from having to pick up parts of the body. He rose in my esteem after that.

Fellow Anti-tank member John Dunlop had witnessed the shocking drama unfold: 'I was the observer for the battery and saw it all happening through the viewer of my range finder in miniature like a film.'

Dunlop's own life was saved at Brunete when the body of a Scottish comrade, John Black, fell on top of him and took a volley of shellfire. As Dunlop peered up, he saw a second body: 'The other man, a runner from a French battalion, was still squatting in the same position, except his head was missing – there was just red flesh round his collar.'[13]

The Spanish Communist Party passbook of John Dunlop, whose life was saved at Brunete when a dying comrade fell upon him and took the blow of a shell.

With such devastation, Battalion morale plummeted. Even Alec Donaldson, involved with propaganda at Albacete and usually tirelessly upbeat, remarked in a post-Brunete letter to Peter Kerrigan:

I was considerably cut up after the Brunete events. The fact our best comrades went 'down' in that offensive upset me tremendously. Brunete was terrible and had all the characteristics of a big battle.

The offensive on Brunete had been an unmitigated disaster for the British Battalion, tactically and in terms of personnel: of 331 men present on the first day of battle, 289 were killed, wounded, or captured by the last. A period of reorganisation was now necessary, and Battalion morale in need of immediate resuscitation.

CHAPTER 4

'Esta noche todos muertos':
Prisoners of Franco

We were taken out once in a while and beaten up. They stood us against the wall and slashed at us with whips. Then we were out back into the dungeons. It was no use protesting. Protests got you nowhere.
Joseph Murray, Glasgow

IN THE SPANISH conflict, International Brigaders were captured in battle and subsequently imprisoned, or worse, with appalling regularity. However, the first Scots to be detained during the conflict were not actually active participants in it. In mid-August 1936, Scottish workers were among those at the British-owned Rio Tinto Company mines near Huelva taken hostage by the pro-republican Miners' Syndicate group. The 36 staff were held inside the mine for almost a fortnight, until nationalists overran the strategically important site and ordered their deportation. Mass arrests and executions of Spanish republican sympathisers among the mine staff followed. One Scot, a Mr Hill, did remain in place at the mine, taking charge of several thousand Spanish workers who were now made to toil for the benefit of Franco's forces, and produce raw materials such as pyrite for export to Nazi Germany.

Individual Scots Brigaders were incarcerated throughout the Spanish war, though two particular occasions saw them detained in large groups. As mentioned above, a significant number, around 30, of the machine-gun company was captured at Jarama, on 13 February 1937. George Watters depicted the moment when in chaotic scenes nationalists surrounded the company and swooped to capture the men:

Finally, they came in from both sides. Someone had cried out that it was our own fellows that were coming up from the rear. We were paying attention to the front. All that I knew about it was that I got hit on the head with the butt end of a rifle. Don Renton was wounded and quite a lot of things had happened. When I came to they were all standing with them with their hands up.

Renton, machine-gun company Political Commissar, gathered himself enough to try and gain military advantage out of the situation:

Prisoners, including Harold Fry, Jimmy Rutherford, Jimmy Maley and Donald Renton, are paraded after their capture at Jarama. The picture was used gloatingly in the anti-republican British press but served only to offer the relatives of missing Brigaders hope.

Our business was to try and mislead the enemy about the actual strength of the Battalion and so build up a conception, when we were being questioned, of an enormous mass of men and materiel there ready to resist fascist onslaught and so on. Harry Fry and I were quite instrumental in building up this picture of a complete wall of opposition, something against which the fascists would be completely destroyed.[14]

The captured were marched towards army trucks for transport to San Martin de la Vega, southwest of Madrid. Tommy Bloomfield, who was alongside Watters, recalled the early moments of capture:

We were tied by our thumbs with field telephone wire in twos and threes and driven behind their lines by Moorish cavalry using the flats of their sabres. To drive us on, Harry Fry [the machine-gun company commander, from Edinburgh] must have been in hell.

Not all the weaponry employed in forcefully escorting the prisoners to their destination was as technologically advanced even as a sword, as Watters continued:

We were passing through a big town when we were going back as prisoners, and there was one fellow who came out with a big club, a prehistoric club, threatening us with this club, shouting at us. I says, 'he's a cheerful bastard!'

During this long procession through what Brigaders nicknamed 'Death Valley', Renton witnessed an incident which would shape his 'militant atheism':

Some of our comrades were dressed in exactly the same way as the fascists, and one of our boys got a very bad one [shot]. He was obviously dying, and a fascist clergyman, one of their chaplains, went forward to this boy to place the cross on his lips. Around him arose the shout 'Rojo! Rojo', meaning, 'Red! Red!', and that crucifix came back before it ever touched the lips of the comrade concerned. Well that is an example of Christian charity. It helps to illustrate how absurd it is for many people to place their faith in whatever kind of religious persuasion they may follow.[15]

At San Martin de la Vega, the arrested men fully expected to be executed, a fear inflamed by the early execution of three of their comrades, including one, Phil Elias of Leeds, who was fatally shot when reaching into his pocket for a cigarette. Tommy Bloomfield told of the moment when another of the company, Ted Dickenson, met his death:

He was given the choice of dying or soldiering for Franco. He chose death. He marched up to a tree like a soldier on parade, did a military about turn saying 'salud comrades' the second he died. What a man! When he was shot, I felt my hair stand on end, my scalp prickle, then my life flashed through my mind, things that had happened to me in my early youth, then a cold sweat and my senses went completely blank.

Jimmy Maley confirmed that the rest of the men anticipated the same fate:

Mr Dickenson was placed three yards away from two soldiers, and when he had given the Spanish salute his brains were blown out. We all thought that we would share the same fate, but the officer in charge of the soldiers marched us away from the spot.

As commander, Harold Fry was at more risk than most, and one of Dickenson's final acts of heroism was to tear Fry's military insignia from his uniform so as to disguise his importance to the company. Fry's own valour during this time was noted by Donald Renton in the *Daily Worker*:

> His broken arm was swinging, and the agonising pain brought beads of sweat to his brow, but even then his quiet words of encouragement helped guarantee us against panic. Forced to watch the cold-blooded murder of Phil Elias and Johnnie Stevens, later the execution of his friend Ted Dickenson, he nevertheless maintained that demeanour which during our period of training and at the front had made him more than simply our military commander. Even the Moors who bound his shattered arm in telegraph wire and beat him up could not make him forego his attitude of quiet contempt towards them.

Thankfully, the captured were given an unlikely reprieve, perhaps when it was realised that they were British combatants and, therefore, potentially of political value. The men were moved on to a prison at Navalcarnero. Renton gave an insight into existence there:

> The Italian fascist officers used to bring their señoritas into the prison to look at the prisoners, and very often to encourage the Moors to come into the cells to knock you about.

From Navalcarnero, the prisoners were transferred to Talavera de la Reina, a concentration camp in the grounds of an old pottery factory southwest of Madrid. Bloomfield continued to fear execution, especially with regular departures from Talavera of the so-called 'agony wagon', a lorry which each day transported 90 republican prisoners to a local graveyard to be shot:

> In the morning when the death wagon had gone they would say to us, '*esta tarde todos muertos*' – this afternoon you all die. When it had gone in the afternoon, we were told '*esta noche todos muertos*' – tonight you all die. Then when that one had gone we would be told '*mañana por la mañana todos muertos*' – tomorrow morning you all die.

Bloomfield and his cellmates subsequently realised that their status as Britons meant they were never likely to be passengers on the agony wagon:

> Then we began to analyse our position. We were under observation when captured so if they executed us there would be reprisals taken in republican Spain. It was a great relief when we realised that.

At Navalcarnero, a triumphant nationalist photo of the shaven-headed prisoners on the back of a truck had been taken, released and published in the British press. On 31 March, the *Daily Mail* reported the Brigaders' capture with a cynicism – not to mention staggering inaccuracy – characteristic of their staunchly pro-nationalist take on the Spanish Civil War:

> These are the first pictures of some of the misguided and hapless British prisoners who were captured by General Franco's forces on the Jarama front. They were sent out to Spain by Communists with promises of work at £6 a week, but the first most of them knew of their real fate was when they were given arms and drafted to the Reds' front line.

Undoubtedly to the chagrin of the right-wing *Mail*, the picture and story brought hope rather than despair; Brigaders' relatives back in Britain had incontrovertible proof that their sons, fathers and husbands were, certainly until recently at least, alive.

The pictures were circulated throughout the media, and during a visit

Jimmy Maley, foreground, and other Brigaders are forced into line after their arrest at Jarama. Maley's mother had images cut from a cinema reel after spotting her son on a Movietone news film.

to the cinema in Paisley, Jimmy Maley's mother was stunned to see her son peering back at her from a British Movietone News film. Such was her relief at learning Maley was in all likelihood still alive, she persuaded the projectionist to cut her two pictures from the reel.

That relatives in Scotland heard little from the prisoners was perhaps a blessing in disguise; so horrific were jail conditions it is unlikely any Brigader would have wanted to worry his family with the truth. In-depth individual interrogation began at Navalcarnero, and Bloomfield was astounded to find that the man interviewing him had a cut glass British accent:

It was a British official who did the interrogating. He had a college education with a Scots accent. His first words were: 'Jolly fine mess you've got yourself into, what?'

This is likely to have been Alfonso Merry del Val, the son of an ex-Spanish Ambassador to London. The prisoners, stated Bloomfield, soon found a cunning route around his questioning:

The 27 of us had been put in three cells. The three cells managed to communicate with each other. A comrade by the name of Bert Levy coached us for when we would be interrogated. Everything he told us to say was the truth, even though it was a pack of lies. Questions and answers were, 'Why did you come to Spain?' 'To do a job of work.' But we didn't add the work was to defeat fascism. 'What happened?' 'After a time they gave us a rifle and a uniform and sent us up the front.' We didn't say we were willing. 'Why didn't you go home?' We replied we had no money and didn't know the language. That was true, so we were never untruthful.

These cross-examinations were often accompanied by physical harassment, as Bloomfield attested:

The first day as a prisoner we had one ration and two bashings from the Germans and Moors. The second day we received two rations and one bashing.

The prisoners were made to live in filthy, unhygienic and cramped surroundings. Bloomfield summed up the foul conditions:

During my three-and-a-half months in prison, I cannot remember having a bath or a wash. Neither did we have a change of clothes. We could pick the body lice off the outside of our trousers they were so plentiful. They were so fat that when you cracked half a dozen between your thumb nails, you had to scrape your nails on the floor to kill more.

In spite of this, felt Donald Renton, morale remained relatively high:

> There were prisoners from not only Britain but from different countries on which the International Brigades were based. Efforts were being made to stimulate ideas of opposition [to the prison guards] between the one group and the other. The general solidarity of the comrades in the concentration camp, to describe it correctly, remained superbly high. Real friendships were built between the different groupings.

In the middle of May 1937, the prisoners were moved from Talavera to the Model Prison at Salamanca. There, they were charged with 'aiding a military rebellion', and made to sit silently through Spanish-language show trials. The men were 'represented' by a nationalist lieutenant, who elected not to speak. Five of the accused, including Harold Fry and Jimmy Rutherford, a young Brigader from Leith, were sentenced to death, and the remaining volunteers to between 20 and 30 years in prison. When Fry was sentenced, Donald Renton later wrote in the *Daily Worker*, 'his shrug of the shoulders was an eloquent testimony to the fact that he could die as Dickenson had died, with his fist clenched and a defiant "*Salud*!"'. George Watters was told that the entirety of his life sentence would be spent in solitary confinement.

Happily, as the internees contemplated their terrifying futures, political negotiations were taking place to secure a mass release, and in late May a prisoner exchange took place, the republicans handing over a group of Mussolini's Italian troops for the release of the men. On 30 May, the British prisoners crossed the Spanish frontier at Irun – where they were made to walk through a crowd of Franco-saluting nationalists – and began their journeys home as free men. At Dover, they were fingerprinted and questioned by the British CID, but released without mention of their being charged under the 1870 Foreign Enlistment Act. In early June, the British government sent its official thanks to Franco for the release of the prisoners.

Despite their experiences, Scots Tommy Bloomfield, Harold Fry, John Hunter, Jimmy Maley, John Montgomery, Jimmy Rutherford, Donald Renton and George Watters all arrived home in Britain keen to return to Spain immediately in order to finish off the fight. For various reasons, a number of them were unable to return: for example, Donald Renton was considered too indispensible to the CPGB to go away once again, while George Watters was extremely ill. Yet nothing could prevent Tommy Bloomfield, Harold Fry or Jimmy Rutherford from going back to Spain less than six weeks after their deportation.

As republican troops hastily retreated from Aragon (see Chapter 14), a second, larger group of British were captured by Italian forces at Calaceite. Over 100 were apprehended on 31 March 1938, with a trickle of further arrests over subsequent days. The new batch of prisoners were taken first to an Italian-run prison camp at Alcañiz, and then on to a military prison at Zaragoza, before their transfer to Burgos, and the infamous camp at San Pedro de Cardeña. Among this group were 36 Scottish Brigaders, including, fatefully, the returning Jimmy Rutherford.

Conditions at San Pedro made Talavera look almost passable in comparison. The camp's international prisoners slept on the floors of dormitories crammed with up to 350 men. Inmate Joseph Murray, a Glaswegian, spoke of the horror of the camp:

> The place was lousy and the food bad. There was no bedding and we slept on the floor with only one blanket. Rats were everywhere. Our prison was a convent from which the nuns had been driven away.

Sanitation was predictably woeful, with one tap shared between 600 men. Open lavatories, often blocked to a height and depth of six feet, made for an overwhelming stench and widespread dysentery. Bouts of scurvy and even malaria were common, with germs carried in the scarce food the prisoners were provided with, and on the omnipresent trinity of mice, lice and fleas.

Regular beatings from the camp's military staff added to the pain of chronically under-treated illness and injury. Inmate William McCartney, another Glaswegian, described how German Gestapo agents used tactics of intimidation, espionage and violence against prisoners, and 'frequent beatings with "loaded" riding whips and rubber hoses'. Inmates were assaulted, too, for failing to take part in what McCartney labelled 'religion with a loaded whip'; in other words, avoidance of enforced mass would trigger severe reprisals. McCartney claimed 95 per cent of prisoners refused to kneel for worship and were accordingly punished. The only light relief for McCartney in San Pedro was the smoking of 'a fine cut up boot lace rolled up in a piece of newspaper'.

Like the Jarama captured, the one thing the imprisoned members of the British Battalion had going for them was their nationality. Such was their value in terms of potential prisoner exchanges, they were unlikely to be executed. In mid-June 1938, after three hellish months at San Pedro, a large number of the British interned were moved to a camp at Palencia ahead of their rumoured exchange for republican-held Italian prisoners.

Conditions in the Italian-run camp at Palencia were marginally better than those at San Pedro, and contact with sympathetic locals brought some solace, as Joseph Murray noted: 'They made us work the land. We got no money and no cigarettes, but the communist element in the town used to smuggle cigarettes to us.' However, Murray explained that attacks on inmates were still a regular occurrence:

We were taken out once in a while and beaten up. They stood us against the wall and slashed at us with whips. Then we were out back into the dungeons. It was no use protesting. Protests got you nowhere.

Finally, on 22 October 1938, confirmation of the prisoner exchange was received, and the British were moved north to San Sebastian, prior to their crossing into France via the international bridge at Hendaye. Nine Scots were in the party of 40 Brits who departed Spain at Irun on 24 October, with the remaining men making the journey over the subsequent week. Despite the privations of life in prison, there was an absence of regret among Scottish Brigaders at their decisions to go and fight. Joseph Murray, speaking to the *Glasgow Herald* on arrival at London Victoria station, summed up the spirit:

I have not heard from my wife for 14 months and now I am looking forward to meeting her and our two children. If it came to the push I would go through the same again.

Unaffected by these group releases, a number of Scots lingered in Spanish prisons until well into 1939. On 7 February of that year, 18 Scots were among 67 British San Pedro veterans released at San Sebastian. Jim Cameron, a fisherman from the Highlands, was not released by Franco until April 1940, making him one of the last foreign prisoners of the war to be freed.

The fates of the three Scots who had been captured at Jarama, repatriated and later returned to Spain differed greatly. As part of the prisoner exchange that had seen them released by the nationalists, the men had signed an agreement stating that if they were ever to return to Spain and be captured, an automatic death sentence would be invoked. They knew, then, that their crossing the Pyrenees into Spain for a second time was a potentially lethal act.

Despite the protestations of his mother, Tommy Bloomfield made it back to Spain and served with distinction on the Aragon Front, before returning home to Kirkcaldy and becoming a family man, 'whose hatred of Franco made him

A Spanish cathedral in Aragon ravaged by shell fire. Close by, a large group of Scottish Brigaders were captured and imprisoned.

live every moment of war in Spain over and over again'.[16]

On re-entering Spain in September 1937, former British Army soldier Harold Fry was made commander of the entire British Battalion. Fry's tenure, though, was to be short-lived, as he was killed during the Battalion's disastrous attempt to capture the village of Fuentes de Ebro the following month. Fry's wife wrote a devastatingly touching tribute to him in a letter to Tom Murray:

My husband went to Spain because he realised the danger of fascism, and believed that his military experience could best be used in fighting it. He joined the International Brigade because he thought it was the job he could do best. His experience of fascist methods of warfare and their brutal treatment of prisoners behind the lines only helped to strengthen his determination to carry on the fight until Franco, Hitler and Mussolini were beaten. This is why he went back to Spain again after a short period of leave, his wound hardly healed, and without ever seeing his baby boy which was born the day after he left. I would not have stopped him even if I could, because I believe he was right, and I'm sure his last thoughts must have been of regret that he could not live to see the final triumph of the forces he fought for.

Disregarding a large age difference, through their shared experiences Jimmy Rutherford and Harold Fry became close friends in Spain. A baby while Fry was serving his country in World War One, Rutherford was a charismatic, highly politicised young volunteer from Newhaven in Leith. His decision to go to Spain, said friend and Labour parliamentary candidate David Dryburgh, 'was no sudden impulse. It was the practical working out of his own theory of life.'

In between his two stints with the British Battalion, Rutherford toured his home area, speaking about what he had seen in Spain. His sister fondly recalled witnessing him holding an audience for one and a half hours at a public hall on Ferry Road, commenting, 'it has never ceased to amaze me how he did it – he wasn't very tall or commanding, but his voice and his vocabulary made up for that.'

Rutherford, though, felt that he could best serve the cause he believed in so passionately by returning to Spain, telling his father, 'if all the young men had seen what I saw out there they would be doing as I am doing.' He returned to Spain in August 1937, and, after being kept back to attend officers' training school for a short time, the Battalion eventually granted Rutherford his wish of rejoining the front line.

Following his arrest at Calaceite in March 1938, aware of the gravity of the situation, Rutherford's comrades attempted to cover for him, and he resolved when questioned to go by the name 'James Small'. What 'Small' could not legislate for was being recognised by Alfonso Merry del Val, who had interviewed him following his apprehension at Jarama and arrived at Zaragoza military prison to perform the same task. The fingerprints Rutherford had given at Jarama merely stood to prove the veracity of Merry del Val's accusation. On 24 May 1938 Jimmy Rutherford was executed by firing squad. He was 20 years old.

Given the difficulty of obtaining accurate news from Spain and its military prisons, similar tales of woe occasionally took a belated twist for the better when genuine facts emerged, as witnessed in Mrs Maley's visit to the cinema.

George Drever, who in his lifetime earned two honours degrees, was listed as having been killed at Belchite. His mother was informed, and she accordingly claimed his death certificate and placed obituary notices in local newspapers, following which Drever's friends in Leith held an emotional memorial meeting. Yet, in July 1938, news that he had been taken prisoner as part of the large group captured in and around Calaceite filtered through. Drever reached his delighted mother's house on 2 November 1938, in her eyes, back from the dead. He regretted greatly that Jimmy Rutherford, his friend from Leith and then San Pedro de Cardeña, was not with him.

Earlier, in November 1936, 19-year-old David MacKenzie was reported to have been killed at University City, Madrid. Back in Scotland, a commemorative service was held for the promising medical student. However, news emerged through the *Daily Worker* on 12 December that MacKenzie was, in fact, alive and well. So ferocious had the nationalist bombardment of his position been, his comrades had presumed him dead. MacKenzie, a first-class gunner, who had reportedly eliminated an entire enemy machine-gun section with one burst of fire, returned to Edinburgh and travelled around Scotland summoning support for the Spanish republic. Such cheerful denouements, however, were rare.

CHAPTER 5

Eating Onions as Apples:
Life as a Volunteer

This place isn't so bad, although it isn't quite as cheerful as Sauchiehall Street on a Saturday evening. As a matter of fact it isn't hellish cheerful at all. You can't drop into Lauder's and have a quiet one and have a night at the Playhouse. As to women, I haven't spoken to one yet. The grub is better than I expected, although there is a lack of meat, sugar, milk etc, but the cigarette shortage more than justified my misgivings which I believe I expressed to you before leaving home. These have to be smoked to be believed, it is absolutely incredible that anyone could brand their contents as tobacco.

John Miller, Alexandria

AS IS FREQUENT in war, participants in Spain spent long periods of inaction behind the front lines of battle. By spring 1937, with the British Battalion bedded firmly in, the organisation of life outside of battle had greatly improved, prompting Jock Cunningham to write on 8 June:

> We have a canteen in the line, a wall newspaper and a trench newspaper, delivered every morning before breakfast. We had a concert up in the line. The lads get bathed regularly, there is plenty of water being brought up by mule. It is possible to get a dozen of the lads to Madrid for two days leave per week. If there is anybody really bad they get 14 days in a rest home in the country.

Political meetings were a staple of communal life in the Battalion. These were overseen by Communist Party-appointed Political Commissars, many of whom were Scottish. Commissars' chief responsibility as far as their duties to volunteers went was keeping up company morale, whether through organising leisure events or giving political instruction.

It is difficult to ascertain to what extent Commissars used political meetings to simply relay the propagandistic messages of the Soviet Union conveyed to them from on high. What can be said is that, on the whole, Commissars felt a great, almost paternalistic devotion to the men they presided over. They were, too, resolutely independent of mind, and it is hard to imagine the likes of Tom

Murray unquestioningly acting as a mouthpiece for Moscow.

Relating what he had witnessed, John Gollan set the scene of a typical political meeting:

> The boys – there were 650 of them, 400 British and 250 Spanish – sat round in a large semi-circle with their rifles across their knees, listening while I explained the situation back home. Imagine it! We could hear the guns very plainly. Lorry-loads of materials for the front and armament convoys kept rumbling by. Overhead, every few minutes, a squadron of planes flew towards the fascist lines. Each time this happened we had to interrupt the meeting because the boys cheered the planes so much.

Peter Kerrigan reported on the content of the meetings:

> Full reports of the situation on all fronts were given, as well as readings from Spanish and British newspapers. These readings and reports gave rise to many useful discussions.

Not all Brigaders were accustomed to the heavily theoretical direction these gatherings often took. Steve Fullarton confessed that one meeting in particular, called by Bob Cooney, left him feeling politically naïve:

> I just listened. We were all sat there, some in the shade, some in the sun, and I just listened to the arguments and it was there I realised what an ignoramus I was, in terms of politics. They were all getting up; somebody over there would quote from Lenin and somebody would quote Marx, and so on. They were quoting by the yard! I thought: 'God help us, how do they know all that?!'

Fullarton's comments suggested that there was an open element to these meetings rather than them being a form of political lecture:

> Sometimes a meeting was what they called a 'beef meeting' – 'beef' was the Yankee way of expressing complaints. It was at such a meeting where you got the complaints off your chest, not that it made much difference!

While the meetings represented a sober form of extracurricular activity, more orthodox forms of entertainment were on offer. George Murray expressed his enthusiasm for a raucous Battalion night:

> We had a concert here last night at which the star songs were such classics

as 'The Old Maid in the Garret' etc!! The good quality of the singing lay mainly in its volume and vehemence!! We also had an 'orchestra' consisting of two mouth-organs and a pipe resembling those used by snake-charmers.

'Fiestas' were regularly held, another highlight for Murray:

We are having a 'fiesta' in the billets tonight and I should very much like you to be present not only to hear my singing (!!), but to witness some of the original, ingenious, weird and wonderful items which will be put across. The humour is always rich and strong on such occasions. By strong I mean that it has to be the opposite of 'parlour'. Notwithstanding that (or maybe because of it) it is always genuine and the laugh is usually against fascism or something else we don't like.

Bill Gilmour spoke of the lift in mood produced by a singing competition held between the different nationalities of the xvth International Brigade. Gilmour sang 'Hame o' Mine' and won a much sought-after shaving kit for his efforts. He felt sure that events such as this helped morale enormously:

We are all as happy as hell in spite of the difficulties of language and customs. That we find it hard to understand one another is more often an attraction than a difficulty. After all, we understand each other spiritually as we are all imbued with the same anti-fascist spirit. We have many a joke at one another's expense due to the many misrepresentations.

The wall newspapers referred to by Jock Cunningham were an extremely popular feature of Battalion life. The papers, mounted on notice boards for all to see, would contain, among other things, useful information, personal news and sketches. George Murray described his Company's version and the charismatic figure behind it, as well as the contentment these activities bred:

The wall newspaper is also worth seeing. We have a unique character who runs it and most of our other 'cultural' activities. In addition to playing a peculiar type of whistle with great skill he writes and produces sketches and 'songs', edits the paper and sets off competitions on everything from military strategy to those which determine whose girl is the best looking. Oh yes, even this life has its compensations. In fact, given its purpose, the compensations greatly outweigh the inconveniences.

Football was played regularly, often between different nationalities. John

During time spent away from the frontlines of battle, Scottish Brigaders fraternise with Spanish, English and Irish comrades.

Gollan refereed a game between the British and Canadian volunteers from the Mackenzie-Papineau Battalion. The Canadians had been challenged by the British to what the latter described as a 'contest in the ancient and honourable traditional game of football as played in Britain'. With coats for goal posts, and 18 players on each side, the match ended 5–4 to the Canadians, thanks mainly to their Spanish 'guest' players (or so their British opponents contended).

Cultural Committees were established, and provided Battalion members with gramophones, wireless radios, draught and chess sets, dominoes and a library. Alec Park glowingly described the latter: 'There is a fine library here, the books and the journals of American labour predominate. The premises used to be the church and now the main building is used for concerts and picture shows.' Lectures were given on various topics, and schools for the education of illiterate Spanish comrades were formed, with lessons given by British soldiers. Brigader Willie McAuley organised a workers' theatre movement, and recorded 'we have written two plays, one dealing with the work of the 5th Column, and the other dealing with International Solidarity.' The establishment of all of this led Bill Gilmour to conclude that 'the health of the Battalion is very good considering everything, and our morale was never better' (tellingly, this was written a month prior to events at Brunete).

Further interest was provided by the visits of public figures such as Clement Attlee and Pandit Nehru, and, perhaps more memorably, Paul Robeson and Errol Flynn. In January 1938, American actor and singer Robeson visited the British Battalion and met a number of Scottish Brigaders, heralding a special relationship with their home country. Robeson was an impassioned supporter of the Spanish republic, and suffered criticism at home for his backing of the American Abraham Lincoln Battalion. In Spain, he sang in Tarazona, and in hospitals at Murcia and Benicassim, announcing of the cause: 'To me, Spain is another homeland because the people are not in favour of racial and class differences.' Alec Park was one of the Scots who saw him sing at Tarazona. Writing in January 1938, he relayed the experience:

> Yesterday afternoon we had the pleasure of a visit from Paul Robeson, his wife, and Charlotte Haldane. Robeson rendered to us many of his songs, but he gave 'Old Man River' to new words, words of hope and struggle and not of as in the past defeatism and helplessness.

Park was to die in battle during the retreat from Aragon, yet Robeson's relationship with the family he left behind lived on. In August 1938, Park's widow, Annie, took her young sons George and Eric to see the singer perform in a concert at City Hall, Glasgow, staged to raise money to send a food ship to republican Spain. The Park family met with Robeson before the performance, and informed him of the death of Alec. As the *Glasgow Herald* reported on 19 August, 'Mr Robeson distinctly recalled meeting Mr Park, and was greatly distressed to learn of his death.' After the concert, Robeson said that because of the atmosphere of solidarity in the auditorium, he had never felt more compelled to sing.

On his visit to Scotland, Robeson revealed a love for the country and in particular the Gaelic language. He visited a clachan in the Western Isles, performing in a village concert hall and later giving an impromptu outdoor performance in Gaelic of 'The Eriskay Love-lilt'.

Annie Park remarried some years later and emigrated to the United States, where, over a decade after meeting him, she attended a Robeson concert held in a private house (it being the McCarthy era, the singer was banned from playing in concert halls or abroad). To her amazement, Robeson spotted her and dedicated a song 'to my friend from Scotland'.

Other Brigaders in Spain were astonished to meet Errol Flynn in Madrigueras. William Jackson and a large group of comrades were enjoying a night in a local bar when the world famous actor walked in and announced: 'The drinks are on me.' Flynn climbed onto a table and, raising a toast to the

British Battalion, vowed: 'If I wasn't Errol Flynn, I'd be fighting with you for your cause.'

One thespian whose fame was yet to come also spent time among Scottish Brigaders. Born in London to Scottish parentage, James Robertson Justice considered himself a Scot, and upon joining the International Brigades must have been heartened to find so many of his compatriots in Spain. Robertson Justice, it is fancifully alleged, escaped the clutches of nationalist troops by pointing at the sky and shouting 'Look! Greylag geese', in the baritone voice that was to become his trademark. An aside perhaps, but interesting to note the link between the Scottish contribution to the Spanish Civil War and *Chitty Chitty Bang Bang*!

In terms of employment conditions, Steve Fullarton and George Watters both remarked that the £1 per week Brigaders were paid proved worthless, as there was simply nothing to spend it on. Of more importance to volunteers was leave, and as Jock Cunningham explained, a system was put in place to ensure occasional periods of recuperation. When on duty at Jarama and Brunete, many Brigaders chose to spend their days off in Madrid, a city suffering intense nationalist bombing. On one of these visits, Bill Gilmour was impressed by the unshakeable Madridleños: 'It was good to sit in a picture house where an unconcerned audience heard the bursting of shells outside, above the dialogue being broadcast for their amusement.'

Despite German bombs raining down on them from 5am to 1pm for the entire three days Gilmour was there, the locals remained impressively unfazed:

> The more I know of the Spanish workers the greater grows my admiration for them. No one regrets the shelling of Madrid more than I. But I am glad that I was able to witness the assets towards the Spanish character that I have herein described. It has been a great tonic to my anti-fascism and by the time I returned to the trenches my hatred for fascism had grown a hundred times greater.

Some leave was spent, understandably, escaping from the pressures of war in local bars. Gilmour explained how easily relief turned to over-indulgence: 'We are still rather unsettled as the exuberance of the boys in their first hours of freedom from the sounds of fire is sometimes carried to excess.'

A more personal pursuit behind the lines was letter-writing and receiving, the latter of which caused Brigaders endless anxieties; some went months without hearing anything from home, such was the predictable unreliability of the wartime postal service. Of almost equal importance to the contents of

Cooks with the Anti-tank Battery photographed at Alcorisa, Aragon, autumn 1937.

letters were the packages accompanying them, and specifically those containing much-cherished British cigarettes. It was rare to find a Scottish Brigader who didn't smoke, and the scarcity and low quality of the cigarettes provided by the republican authorities was legendary. Alec Donaldson summed up the problem:

> The smokes problem is very acute. We sometimes get one packet per week of cigarettes which have only one claim to the name, the fact that they have the same shape as the genuine article. They are known as 'anti-tanks' and are twice as deadly.

Glaswegian Thomas McWhirter described the lengths stretched to in desperation for tobacco:

> We have started Butting Clubs. One must be quick on the draw to tap an after nowadays. I saw a comrade smoke nut shells today. Personally my worst attempt has been at tree leaves; they are not so bad.

Though volunteers were short of cigarettes to puff on after meals, food itself was an important issue during the Spanish conflict. Political Commissar

Bob Cooney, a late arrival in September 1937, having been retained in Scotland for his importance to the CPGB, laconically emphasised the importance of nutrition to the Battalion quartermaster Robert 'Hooky' Walker: 'Feed the boys well and they'll fight well.' Alec Park detailed the meal-time experience:

> The meals are, roughly, coffee at 7.30am, lunch about 1.30pm and supper about 6.30pm. The food is mainly soups and beans and rice and I feel I am doing fairly well on it although the cup of tea is missing.

In terms of ingredients and quantities, the culinary experiences of Brigaders appear to have varied greatly, in line with which period they were in Spain, and in which position they found themselves. David Anderson, at one time platoon commander in the Mackenzie-Papineau Battalion, recalled in desperate hunger eating snakes and snails, while Edinburgh student David MacKenzie's diet consisted of three main staples: rice, beans and chick-peas. On the Aragon Front, Tommy Bloomfield became so hungry that he began to eat raw onions as if they were apples, a habit he continued for the rest of his life. Steve Fullarton admitted of the Battle of the Ebro: 'We were always hungry and food probably was our main topic of conversation.'

However, this ravenousness was usually more of an issue on the front line; satisfaction with rations behind the lines seems to have been general. George Murray observed that 'the food here is plain and wholesome and agrees with my stomach', and added that any hunger pangs could be defeated by eating oranges, apples and cherries plucked from the trees. His brother Tom, in April 1938 a very late arrival, was more than pleased with the menu:

> I just returned from supper, 7pm. Our menu consisted of soup, rissoles, bread, chocolate, a peach, coffee. 'Six course', you might say, but of course you understand that the courses are not large.

George Watters recognised that in the circumstances, the Brigaders ate well:

> We were pretty fortunate as far as food was concerned at that particular time. Despite the difficulties that were there we seemed to get just enough to do us, and alongside of that we weren't looking for much. We knew that certain things had to be for the Spanish children. And because of that I never heard a complaint yet regarding the food.

There was even scope for the occasional celebratory meal; a Burns Supper was held close to the Jarama Valley in 1937, with potatoes, sardines, songs and poetry the order of an evening attended by 1,000 republican soldiers. At the year's end, Bill Gilmour enjoyed a Christmas feast:

> We had a marvellous dinner on Christmas Day. We managed to buy four chickens, and to rustle some potatoes and dried fruit. A Greek roasted our chickens and cooked our spuds, so the cooking and preparation had the quality 'par excellence'. Chickens and beef with mashed potatoes, Christmas pudding, compressed fruit and nuts, oatcakes, French cheese, tea, Malaga wine and cognac. It will remain one eternal sweet memory.

'Vino' was a thankfully frequent pleasure for the non-teetotal element of the Scottish contingent (given the national reputation, this group was not as large as might be expected; Tom Murray was joined in abstinence by Steve Fullarton, Tommy Bloomfield and many more). However, some Scots missed a more traditional tipple, as Eddie Brown wrote in a letter home to Perth: 'That's one thing I would like just now, a pint of beer. We cannot get beer out here. We were never boozers, but we liked our pint.'

John Dunlop, who found himself in a spot of bother when he and a group of comrades siphoned wine from the barrels of a cellar in an abandoned village, recalled the trouble alcohol could cause by citing one particular event. Barney Shields, an ex-British Army regular who had served in India, had spent an evening enjoying the local grape in Mondejar, where the Battalion were situated for post-Brunete training in advance of their move into Aragon. Despite being drunk, Shields was asked to guard Battalion headquarters for the night. Patrolling, he noticed that Political Commissar Walter Tapsell, a disciplinarian loathed by many in the Battalion, had left his high-laced leather boots outside the bedroom door as he slept. The temptation proved too much for Shields, and, Dunlop remembered, he duly 'relieved himself inside them, filled them to the brim. Tapsell got up the next morning and put his foot in. Just as he had been

George Murray, right, and two comrades enjoy a 'rest day' away from the harsh realities of frontline action.

thinking as to what grand exhortations he would offer the troops that day, he plunged in his left foot.' As punishment, Shields was put into the 'digger', a form of prison cell burrowed into the ground, though, noted Dunlop, it didn't bother him as his awestruck comrades passed bottles of wine through the bars. Shields, it should be noted, was an outstanding marksman with the machine-gunners, and was to die a defiant and valorous death at Belchite.

Over consumption of alcohol was not a problem unique to the International Brigades. Ethel MacDonald, in Spain as a representative of the anarchist United Socialist Movement (see Chapters 11, 12 and 13), found that volunteers to POUM-associated militia groups were also regularly over-indulging in Spain, as she verified in a diary entry for 14 January 1937:

Charlie Doran is sitting here at present telling me all about Glasgow and Lanarkshire. He came the day before yesterday with the ILP section from London and he is attached to the POUM. Why does someone not impress on the British volunteers not to get drunk when they arrive here? There is always that tendency. Perhaps it is because they are unaccustomed to wine. Doran was very indignant at the idea of volunteers for freedom getting drunk, and I sympathise with his feelings.

Clearly, this perceived excessiveness did not meet with universal approval, though the impact of alcohol on the British Battalion or on the militias was never significantly debilitating.

Hygiene, cleanliness and health were obviously difficult to maintain in the wartime countryside. Alec Park wrote from Aragon in February 1938 itemising the intricacies of dealing with lice:

This morning has been spent 'de-lousing'. The process is as follows. All our clothing and blankets are put through a machine built on a motor chassis. It is a boiler affair and when the container is filled with stuff to be 'de-loused', the container is pushed back into the boiler and closed with locking screws. Steam is then injected into the boiler also a chemical which does the killing of the louse. Whilst this is going on we of course are all without clothes but are given a sponge down with alcohol to give the louse on us the 'once-over'. Further the rooms where we sleep and our mattresses are chemically treated. The process of de-lousing is pretty thorough and any louse that lives through it would I believe have to caught and shot!

Whether through disease from these conditions or, as was far more likely, battle wounds, British Battalion members would be hospitalised in what were usually makeshift units in former hotels, churches and other large buildings. Though there was an acute lack of medical staff and equipment, and conditions especially in early-war hospitals could be horrendous, in the context of war some of the improvised facilities provided outstanding care in pleasant surroundings. George Murray, who for several months following a shot wound had been 'missing', forcing his nurse sister Annie to trawl the medical centres of republican Spain looking for him, described the surroundings he later found himself in:

A defiant George Murray following his arrival at hospital in Huete, where he joined his nurse sister Annie.

I get plenty of varied food and fruit to satisfy my hunger. We are well looked after and there are German doctors who know their business. This is a lovely place built for the indulgence of fastidious aristocrats but admirably suited to the needs of their convalescent enemies! There is a river nearby, shady trees and fine high buildings with big verandas and flat roofs where we can sunbathe.

Willie McAuley, wounded at Brunete, reported to Peter Kerrigan that his own hospital was well-organised and functioned along co-operative lines:

I am in the British hospital, and the treatment is very good. The hospital has been converted from an ancient convent, and when one enters the place, he is immediately struck with the alterations. The happy buzz of conversations in the wards among comrades, the majority of whom are in pain, speak themselves for the efficient running of the hospital. The organisation of the hospital in regard to social and cultural life is very good. We have our own band, composed of wounded comrades and we run dances. We have an excellent recreation room, complete with canteen, library, games etc. We are visited once a week by a travelling film show. It would be difficult for people in Great Britain to understand how our hospital is run. We have no artificial separation between the medical staff and the patients. One and all have the same interest, how can we improve the hospital, and because of this we have built a hospital we are very proud of.

Though these hospitals were obviously well run, nothing could hide the fact that they contained patients with extreme war wounds. Before his stay in the more salubrious hospital described above, George Murray shared a ward with some profoundly unfortunate victims of the conflict:

There was one fellow lying across from me with his head more or less half off. The blokes used to go along and lift up the cloth that he was in and have a look at him. The Spaniards were very insensitive, as far as that was concerned. I was amazed to see this Swiss coming through from one room to another, walking on his hands. He had a wound on his legs.[17]

Following an injury suffered at Brunete, Bill Gilmour wrote from hospital detailing the horrors inflicted on his fellow patients:

It is here one sees those who have suffered for the cause. Broken bodies, disfigured features, limbless heroes, who are useless for an active life in the future. When I look to them, I observe my own wounds with contempt, as mere pin pricks compared to what they must have suffered.

As Gilmour himself had found out, receiving treatment on the battlefield and in these hospitals could be perilous. He recounted his own desperate tale in a letter home of July 1937:

I have been very ill, but it is over I hope, and during the times when I was able to write I was instilled with such a fit of melancholy that I could write nothing but a screech of misery such as was unfit to send anyone. My wounds are pretty well healed up now, but the effects of the anti-tetanus injection were what did the dirty work. The anti-tetanus injection was administered in the field, and for the first five days in hospital, I had nothing to worry about except my wounds. Then without the slightest warning, my body broke out all over in a rash; great white blotches all over my body. It irritated like hell. I could have scratched the skin from my flesh. My tongue swelled to twice its size. Also my hands and feet. My head split and my stomach grew so disordered that everything I ate was almost immediately vomited up again. I got over that spasm and I had not been two days when the whole thing happened all over again.

With so much rusting, dilapidated equipment in use, there was an atrocious inevitability about such illnesses being contracted. Though the republican side clearly achieved much in providing healthcare, a lack of resources left them with some extremely primitive facilities unfit for use in times of war or peace. A positive aspect of the hospital experience was the way in which it allowed members of the British Battalion to mix with locals, something difficult to do on the often rural front lines of war. Indeed, many, such as Steve Fullarton, picked up their only Spanish while convalescing.

Some opportunities to spend time with Spaniards behind the lines did exist. Like many other Scots Brigaders, George Murray found a welcoming people but was staggered by their poverty:

The people here are likeable and friendly and they look quite healthy and well fed. Their houses and mode of life, however, appear to have changed little for centuries. The majority of the people in this district are peasant.

In contrast to Steve Fullarton, Murray did find time to take Spanish lessons in between stints at the front, though with mixed results. Unfortunately, the rudimentary Spanish of Murray and his colleagues made charming local members of the opposite sex difficult:

We have a Spanish class and I am now a fluent linguist. My Spanish is so perfect that the Spaniards hardly understand a word I am saying! The Spanish people are very attractive and not as squalid as I expected. They are friendly and happy whenever they have the least excuse. The children are pretty and intelligent and the girls ditto! Unfortunately we are handicapped in that we cannot speak to them much, plus the fact that some actions of our predecessors have led to a widespread suspicion of our intentions!

There was, too, a certain amount of assimilation with Spanish life in other elements of Brigader existence. Murray was in a party of Brigaders that attended a bullfight, though he was left somewhat underwhelmed:

We saw six bulls baited and killed. The spectacle was not particularly exciting and it didn't even look so disgusting as one would expect. The matadors are very clever, of course, and their foot work was a study, but only Spaniards can really appreciate the fine points about the sport.

Despite his comfort in Spain and a burgeoning love of the country, Murray did later admit a hankering for his homeland:

I wouldn't mind a glimpse of Perth just now if only for the green colour of the Inches and hills that are not bare and white for lack of water. Now I understand people who come from hot climes and marvel at the green landscape of Scotland.

There were a number of home comforts to be enjoyed while adjusting to the local way of life, however. Jimmy Moir delighted in a visit to a village cinema where he witnessed, in equal bemusement to the locals, a Soviet film entirely in Russian. Moir noted the audience's worship of Joseph Stalin, perceived as a kind benefactor to the republican cause:

Whenever Stalin appeared on the screen the Spaniards got up and shouted red slogans. It reminded me of the silent films of 10 years ago when the audience shouted advice to the hero when he was in danger, and cheered the downfall of the villain of the piece.

Bill Gilmour appeared charmed by that same excitable nature of the Spanish citizens, and in particular the ebullience of the children:

We are billeted in a schoolhouse in a little village not far from Madrid. The children are not to be ousted so easily however, they still look upon this school as their own property in spite of the fact we have obtained possession. We have a hell of a job trying to keep their little inquisitive fingers from our arms. The little girls use our passages for skipping in, and they can't skip without holding a community sing song. The boys spend their time either cadging our cigarettes or going to fill our water bottles 'for a consideration!' I find it all very pleasant however and interesting too.

While Jimmy Moir witnessed a spontaneous airing of political views in the cinema, Alec Park found a more formal display of loyalties:

The people are solid and you are greeted on all sides with 'Salud camarada' even by the children. They have been celebrating Lenin's birthday, in the market square there is a large picture of Lenin on a red banner, at night there is lit up a large red star and all around the balconies of the buildings display pictures of the various Soviet and Spanish republican leaders amidst the republican colours.

Such devotions chimed happily with those of Park and many of his comrades, meaning shared politics became a useful tool of assimilation.

The British Battalion's 'grub truck', which was at one stage rescued from outside a local brothel.

Unity was also achieved on a more human level. Tommy Bloomfield often talked warmly of the reception he and his fellow volunteers received in small villages, and recalled how impoverished Spaniards would give their visitors every scrap of food they could muster. In turn, Bloomfield and company would regularly pretend to have already eaten, and accordingly return the food. His own admiration for the Spanish people was cemented when he witnessed three women pull a grounded fascist pilot from a tree and forcibly detain him.

There did exist some problems between volunteers and the indigenous population. Hamish Fraser, during the civil war an influential member of the Spanish Communist Party's secret police, the Servicio de Inteligencia Militar (SIM), and yet by 1970 a Conservative councillor in Saltcoats, discharged himself early from hospital because of the hostility within:

> I was hospitalised in Barcelona after having been wounded at Seguro de Baños on 16 February 1938. Such was the atmosphere there at that time I volunteered to return to the front before my wound had healed and, paradoxically, felt much safer there.

The behaviour of some Brigaders did occasionally upset the locals and make gaining acceptance difficult. Peter Kerrigan wrote to Harry Pollitt shortly before the Battle of Jarama to inform him that a driver with the field kitchen had taken the 'grub truck' used for food supplies when drunk. The vehicle was recovered outside a brothel, while its driver lingered within.

These, though, appear to have been extremely isolated incidents. Scots Brigaders found, on the whole, a heartfelt welcome and immense gratitude from Spaniards, and behaved with a deep respect for the country and its people. Many fell in love with Spain, and spent the Franco era dreaming of a return. The prevailing attitude of Spanish natives and of volunteers was summed up by Brigader James Wark, a World War One veteran from Airdrie:

> This is something different from the last war. We know what we are fighting for this time. The kiddies hold up their hands in the Red Front Salute and greet us as we pass. I'm proud to be fighting for the Spanish people and democracy.

Rarely before or since were foreign soldiers so welcome in another country's war.

CHAPTER 6

With the Best of Intentions:
The Scottish Ambulance Unit

The work already carried out by these Scotsmen who came to Spain to
mitigate the sufferings of war is really extraordinary.
Politica, Spanish newspaper

THE FIRST ORGANISED group of people who left Scotland to intervene in
Spain's war did not travel with the aim of joining the fighting. The Scottish
Ambulance Unit (SAU) left Glasgow on 17 September 1936. The idea of sending
such a unit was the brainchild of Daniel MacAuley Stevenson, an 85-year-
old ex-Lord Provost of Glasgow, and from 1934 the Chancellor of Glasgow
University. At the start of hostilities in Spain, Stevenson brought together an
Executive Committee to discuss the idea of sending over a medical company
that would assist wounded combatants on both the nationalist and republican
sides. Largely consisting of sympathetic members of the upper class such as the
Marchioness of Aberdeen and the Countess of Oxford and Asquith, the group
launched itself from an office at 5 Cleveden Road, Glasgow, and immediately
began the search for the funds, staff and equipment required. Fundraising
activities were quickly organised, and an appeal for volunteer drivers, medical
students and doctors initiated.

Though Stevenson himself often appeared sympathetic to the Spanish
republic, his reputation was tainted by a distant relationship with the Nazi
regime in Germany. Visitors to his Glasgow office such as Dr Len Crome
recalled seeing a portrait of Adolf Hitler on Stevenson's desk, and in late 1937
the educationalist accepted a medal for his services to a German–Scottish
exchange programme, the citation for which read:

> The Chancellor of the German Reich, Herr Hitler, has bestowed on Sir
> Daniel MacAuley Stevenson the Cross, first class, of the Meritorious
> Order of the German Eagle in recognition of Sir Daniel's foundation
> some years ago of exchange scholarships between Scottish and German
> students.

Perhaps ironically therefore, Stevenson faced criticism from the right
rather than the left for his central involvement with the SAU. Glasgow Bailies

Victor D Warren and John Murdoch condemned the idea of Stevenson's SAU as dangerously contrary to the government's policy of neutrality, with Warren contending that 'private intervention is even worse than political intervention'.

The import of these criticisms was that the SAU had been set up primarily to aid the republican wounded in Spain. The Executive Committee was forced to release a statement re-avowing the SAU's commitment to neutrality once it reached Spain, stating:

> The duties of such a mobile unit must of necessity assume a most varied character in rendering aid where and when necessary to the casualties resulting from fighting, irrespective of party, and to sick and wounded members of the non-combatant population.

Eschewing these political squabbles, the people of Glasgow had set about raising funds for the SAU with zest. 'Flag Days' were staged, while the local branch of the Musicians' Union offered to supply a symphony orchestra for a fundraising concert, and the Glasgow Trades Council pledged its backing. This enthusiastic support was to continue in the city and across Scotland for the duration of the Unit's stay in Spain.

Members of the SAU witnessed this support first hand, when a large crowd turned out to wave them off from Glasgow's George Square on 17 September. The khaki-clad crew of 19 people drove six ambulances to Dover, and then onwards through France to Marseilles, where they caught a steam boat to Barcelona. They were led by Fernanda Jacobsen, a formidable, middle-aged Scottish woman proudly dressed in a kilt and sporting a Glengarry bonnet.

The SAU staff, all but two of whom were Scottish, was pitched straight into work in Spain. Unit member WL Freebairn, of Kilsyth, described their involvement in an October 1936 republican retreat from Olias del Rey northwards towards Illescas, as the ambulances struggled to carry wounded people to hospital in the face of a nationalist advance:

> The effect of the advance was to demoralise the republicans. The republican militia, mixed in indescribable confusion with women and children, fled terror-stricken before the Moors and their modern weapons. Some of the women and children were assisted by the ambulances to get to places of safety. There were touching scenes when men, howling with fear, grabbed on to the sides of the ambulances and pleaded to be taken.

Despite the regularity of bombs dropping all around them, Freebairn and

The second Scottish Ambulance Unit, led by the kilted Fernanda Jacobsen, are given a send off by the Lord Provost of Glasgow, John Stewart, on 17 January 1937. Unit member George Burleigh, second from the left, and three of his colleagues would soon incense Jacobsen by resigning their posts with the ambulance.

his colleagues worked tirelessly on that Toledo front and, indeed, wherever they were dispatched in Spain. Fernanda Jacobsen contacted Daniel Stevenson with news of their good work on 28 October, cabling the words: 'All working at high pressure. The Embassy and the Spaniards say ambulance doing magnificently.' Locally, such was their perceived value, the Unit had earned the nickname 'Los Brujos' – The Wizards.

However, all was not as it seemed with the SAU. Two weeks prior to the sending of the above telegram, seven members of the Unit had been sent home, two for perfectly legitimate health reasons, the other five 'as a disciplinary measure'. The five men had been placed under house arrest in Madrid's National Hotel by Duncan Newbigging, Unit commander, and then sent to Alicante to board a ship for Marseilles. They stood accused of looting the bodies of soldiers on the battlefield and ransacking abandoned properties, charges they vigorously denied in an official statement released on their arrival in London. The five claimed that the charges had been fabricated as a reaction to their refusal to hand over the keys of six of their ambulances to local militias.

On 17 October, the returnees were summoned to an enquiry meeting presided over by Daniel Stevenson and attended by members of the SAU's Executive Committee. After four hours of submissions, the meeting was adjourned with no conclusions reached.

Presented at the enquiry had been a sensational and incriminating statement from Hugh Slater, later Chief of Operations for the entire XVth Brigade. He claimed that one of the SAU five, Donald Perfect, had come to him in Madrid and given an account of their arrest by the Spanish authorities, and his own subsequent escape. Perfect had then stated that he would not be returning to Britain because of the riches on offer in Spain. He went on to describe as 'mementoes' the valuables SAU members had taken in Spain, and listed the contents in his own kitbag as:

1. A solid gold crucifix between nine inches and a foot long
2. Some gold ornaments taken off a decanter
3. Three gold and amber ashtrays
4. A set of silver fish knives.

Slater then listed 'souvenirs' claimed by other SAU members:

One had a thick roll of French bank-notes found in a house in Aranjuez where they were billeted. At least two had taken revolvers from dead or wounded militiamen (the Unit is not authorised to carry arms). My informant and another member of the Unit had spent the afternoon of the day before their arrest digging in the cellar of their headquarters, looking for the jewels of the previous owner of the house which they had been told were buried there.

Slater had immediately reported his discoveries to the Communist Party, and later heard that the men had been deported, having been detained by the British authorities rather than their Spanish counterparts, as Perfect had alleged. At the end of his statement, Slater somewhat menacingly reminded the SAU Executive that 'The usual practice in Spain is to shoot looters without trial.'

Fortunately for the five accused, the Executive Committee did not wield such powers of summary justice, and the matter was, seemingly, allowed to slip. The controversy did not detract from Glaswegians' enthusiasm for the SAU, and in the same month a Spanish market was held in the Central Halls to raise much-needed funds – the Executive required at that point a further £9,000 to avoid the immediate withdrawal of the Unit from Spain. Neither was praise for their work in Spain difficult to find, with even the seemingly pro-nationalist foreign secretary Anthony Eden praising the SAU's work in republican Spain on 18 December. In their first months in Spain, estimated Fernanda Jacobsen, the

SAU had treated 2,500 wounded and helped transport 1,000 evacuees, a fine achievement given the controversy that dogged them in that period.

Tired and low on equipment, the remaining members of the first SAU returned to Scotland towards the end of 1936. Daniel Stevenson announced that a second Unit could only be sent to Spain if £5,000 was swiftly raised. Following events in Spain, they were in dire need of new staff and apparatus, as the *Glasgow Herald* confirmed on 21 December:

> Little by little, the personnel dwindled down to two, the men having had to return home on account of shellshock, physical and mental pain, and other causes. Two of them were caught with their ambulance by the insurgents, one further ambulance was burned, and thus the original equipment of six ambulances and one store wagon was reduced to four ambulances and one wagon.

Regular opponents of the SAU saw these weaknesses as a chance to call for the abandonment of its work in Spain. Bailie Warren was again the principal critic, writing to the *Glasgow Herald* to express his hope that the SAU had 'come home to stay home'. Their presence in Madrid, he wrote, 'is to be interpreted as sympathy with the Socialists and Anarchists in Spain who have desecrated and destroyed all forms of religion.' Warren's claim that 'it is the wish of the largest population of Daniel Stevenson's fellow citizens that his ambulance unit does not return to Spain' was shown to be dubious when popular support and not a little help from the Lord Provost of Glasgow bolstered the SAU to the extent that it was soon ready for a return to action. On 17 January 1937, the replenished SAU set off for Spain again. It comprised two new ambulances and supply wagons, and a small emergency car. The second SAU had 11 staff in all, three from the original mission including Fernanda Jacobsen, seven new Scots and an English doctor, Len Crome.

They arrived in Madrid to find a city now ravaged by the effects of relentless nationalist air bombardments. Jacobsen wrote to Daniel Stevenson in the second week of February giving an account of conditions:

> Starvation is rampant, and neither for love nor money is a bit of coal to be had in Madrid. Everyone looks pinched and miserable. We cannot get any food to buy here for ourselves so we have to draw on our relief supplies to feed the unit, no matter how frugally, and then deal with relief work. The people are literally starving, and babies are dying for want of milk.

As well as medical work, the SAU devised a chit system on behalf of local authorities through which it could distribute food supplies to the neediest residents. Their indefatigable work provoked high praise from Madrid's *Politica* newspaper:

> There could hardly be a combatant of these days who has not seen and admired the khaki uniforms of the stretcher-bearers, blending with the canvas of the ambulances, moving to and fro near the firing line. The work already carried out by these Scotsmen who came to Spain to mitigate the sufferings of war is really extraordinary.

The SAU's constant proximity to the front line meant they regularly endured close shaves with stray artillery. Unit member Morris Linden was evacuating wounded soldiers from behind the lines at Jarama when an air raid began:

> About 40 bombs were dropped by one aeroplane within a short distance of the ambulance. One bomb landed in a field within 25 yards of the ambulance. Had it fallen on the hard road instead of in the soft clay-like ground of the field, this bulletin would have contained much more serious news.

On 12 May, the SAU was present on the Toledo front during an air attack by nationalist forces, which lasted 45 minutes. Though the seven crew members were able to dive for cover and cram into a two-person air raid dugout, their four ambulances suffered great damage.

Bombs were not the only element of Unit life causing the Executive Committee back in Scotland consternation. On 12 April, Daniel Stevenson issued a statement to refute press allegations that the SAU was on its way home due to mutiny in the ranks. Any trouble there had been, he wrote, was merely 'bickering' among two or three SAU staff. Yet there had been more to it than mere bickering.

In March, Unit members Dr Len Crome, Roddy MacFarquar, Maurice Linden and George Burleigh had resigned from the SAU and joined the Spanish Medical Aid Committee's International Brigade team. Prior to the stalemate at Jarama, they had been appalled when Fernanda Jacobsen had suggested that, in the event of the nationalists advancing and successfully surrounding Madrid, the SAU should remain in place to help their wounded. Conversely, the four felt that the SAU should stay behind republican lines and hand their food supplies over to the government authorities if Madrid were to become surrounded.

Refusing to accept their resignations, a furious Jacobsen took them for what she hoped would be an admonishment from the British consul in Madrid.

Members of the second Scottish Ambulance Unit. Left to right: M Linden (Glasgow), R MacFarquhar (Inverness), A Boyd (Bearsden), J MacKinnon (Ayr), G Burleigh (Kilsyth), T Penman (Glasgow), T Watters (Tillicoultry) and unidentified.

He, though, was a sympathetic republican, and wished the men luck in the Brigades. Jacobsen returned to her depleted Unit incandescent with rage.

Perhaps unsurprisingly, given these events, Jacobsen and the four remaining members of the Unit were back in Scotland by the end of July (a further two had earlier returned home injured). Officially, the Unit had returned for an equipment refit while the Spanish Civil War was deadlocked. Privately, there was some doubt as to whether it would return for a third stint.

By September, with a further financial boost from local fundraising efforts and a successful recruitment drive, those doubts were extinguished. For the third time, on 2 September 1937 the SAU set off for Spain, its crew of seven Scots and an Englishman small but unfaltering in their commitment, as symbolised by the continued presence of Tillicoultry man Tom Watters.

Again, there was some condemnation of the Unit from anti-republicans, who, despite Daniel Stevenson's repeated assertions that the SAU was a neutral organisation, continued to claim it was a servant of the Spanish government. A correspondent going by the name of 'Right and Reason' wrote in the *Glasgow*

Herald of 29 September that: 'It is a matter of regret to me and to many others that a Scottish Ambulance Corps has been sent to one side only, and that the side of misrule.'

Nevertheless, the third SAU remained in Spain until July 1938, at which point Unit vehicles and equipment were transferred to the republican authorities in Madrid. On their return to Glasgow, some of the Unit's longest servants expressed their exasperation with the war. Tom Watters admitted to the *Glasgow Herald* that he and many other non-combatants were now 'fed up' with conditions in Spain.

A further controversial allegation concerning the SAU was that its ambulances were used to transport anti-republican Spaniards out of Madrid. In return, it was suggested, obliging SAU crew members would be rewarded handsomely with personal gifts.

Rumours of this duplicitous behaviour had been an additional influence on the decision of Roddy MacFarquhar and his three colleagues to resign from the SAU. MacFarquhar in particular had been suspicious of Fernanda Jacobsen's friendship with Captain Edwin Lance, a staunch anti-communist known for arranging the escape of pro-Francoists from government territories. MacFarquhar noted how Jacobsen always seemed to meet with Lance 'after any visits made to and at the fronts – which I personally did not like at all.'[18] Tellingly, on 8 October 1937, Lance was arrested by republican police and imprisoned indefinitely for aiding nationalist escapees. Jacobsen and some of her unit had, it would seem, elected to apply their own version of the SAU's avowed neutrality.

However, the SAU did carry out valiant work in treacherous circumstances and its achievements were impressive. Additionally, the Scottish movement to raise an ambulance unit had the notable side effect of unifying Establishment figures with local left-wing activists in the name of one cause. But, perhaps buckling under the strain and contradictions of trying to avoid partisanship in a time of war, it was often overwhelmed by controversy, its good name forever sullied by murky allegations.

CHAPTER 7

Red Nightingales:
Nursing Volunteers

They need our help, poor people, and if you only could see them when
bombs are dropping overhead. I can vouch your heart would ache. Mothers
snatch their children and run madly for shelter. Again, they are starving
Sister Winifred Wilson, St Andrews

FURTHER SCOTTISH MEDICAL aid in Spain came from volunteer nurses, inspired
on humanitarian and political grounds to serve in the conflict.

Margot Miller, a 24-year-old nurse born in Stirlingshire, was one of the first
medical volunteers to arrive in Spain. Miller worked with the Red Cross on
the Aragon Front, and ended up a casualty herself due to nationalist machine-
gun fire. As she explained:

Four of us were walking across a field between the trenches when our
Red Cross uniforms were observed and a machine-gun was turned on
us. A German guide was shot through the neck and I was wounded in
both legs.

In an unexpected role-reversal, the young nurse was stretchered off to
hospital by Spanish militiamen. Despite this, like so many other Scottish
volunteers in Spain who had suffered setbacks, she remained steadfast in her
determination, pledging from her sick bed, 'I hope to return to Spain in about
a fortnight. I am just waiting for my legs to heal.'

Sister Winifred Wilson, a St Andrews woman and founder member of the
College of Nursing, arrived in Spain in January 1937 to join the British section
of the Spanish Medical Aid Committee's International Brigade unit. She
worked at first in an operating theatre, and then on hospital wards. Wilson's
unit had to be extremely mobile, packing equipment on sudden command and
travelling wherever assistance was most needed. Rarely was her work carried
out in actual hospitals; improvisation was a key asset for medical staff, as
Wilson highlighted in April 1937, when writing to friends in Kirkleod that
'we are in a small village, and the town hall is my ward, and the ante-room is
the operating theatre'.

In the same letter, she described the horror she had witnessed, espousing a familiar view on British non-intervention:

> After an attack we are working day and night. Oh, if you only saw the slaughter! Heads and faces blown to bits, stomachs and brains protruding, limbs shattered or off. I never met such bricks of lads. Every company has been simply slaughtered. I wish Britain had helped at first and prevented such a massacre. I cannot think why we have not tried to stop it all.

Wilson recognised that she and her nursing colleagues were now part of the Spanish republican army, who could not 'depart from Spain until the end of the war', though this was not a challenge she was about to shirk:

> They need our help, poor people, and if you only could see them when bombs are dropping overhead. I can vouch your heart would ache. Mothers snatch their children and run madly for shelter. Again, they are starving.

As members of the International Brigade, Wilson's unit were seen as a legitimate target by nationalist aeroplanes, and despite their earlier misses, she had no doubt that 'they mean to get us yet'. Regardless of this, the defiant nurse wrote, 'I have no regrets that I came to help'.

Of the three Murray siblings who served in Spain, Annie was the first to volunteer. She arrived there in late September 1936, and was to serve for almost the entire duration of the war. Born in Aberdeenshire in 1906, Annie came from an extremely politicised family and had led protests against working conditions while employed at the Edinburgh Royal Infirmary. It was perhaps unsurprising, therefore, that she chose to put her burgeoning nursing career on hold and volunteer for Spain through the British Medical Aid Committee. In her eyes, the decision to go to Spain was straightforward:

> I went to Spain because I believed in the cause of the Spanish republican government. I didn't believe in fascism and I had heard many stories of what happened to people who were under fascist rule.[19]

On arrival, Murray was sent to work in the Primere Unidad Ingles hospital in Grañen, near Huesca on the Aragon Front. The hospital had been paid for by the Spanish Medical Aid Committee in Britain, though it contained both native and international patients. An early task for Murray and her colleagues was to make the run-down hospital functional:

Annie Murray, centre, takes part in the vital work of preparing bandages for reuse.

The hospital was a very old building, badly in need of repair. The unit got working together to make it a fit place in which to nurse the wounded. The yard was very dirty and bad-smelling, and had to be drained and levelled after many loads of refuse had been removed. We worked at these and other improvements between each attack, so that even if the front was quiet we were always busy.

At Grañen, she was impressed to see female soldiers taking part in military actions: 'There are many women in the army here and they appear exactly like men when they come in from the front. I think some of them are very brave.'

This was to be one of the few comforting sights of her experiences. Murray had to treat the most harrowing of injuries. Despite being republican-run, the hospitals she worked in treated the wounded of both sides during the conflict, and one of the earliest wounded combatants she saw was a Moorish nationalist soldier, brought to the hospital after having lain injured on the battlefield for five days:

His broken, lacerated leg was literally crawling with maggots. The poor devil was so frightened, not knowing what he was coming to, but we tried to the best of our ability to assure him that he was here to have his wound treated and generally cared for. Unfortunately we had to amputate his leg immediately but he died the next day.

By late October 1936, Murray, in one of her regular letters home to the family, wrote how the paucity of hospital equipment available meant seriously ill people were being discharged to make room for new arrivals. As the war intensified, so did the quantity of patients and her frustration at inaction from Britain:

We have had an extremely busy and rather a depressing time at hospital here lately. We have been taking all kinds of cases and I can tell you we have had many very tragic ones amongst them and many deaths. Many have been shot through the lungs and heads, many legs, arms, abdomen and other injuries. Few of the lung and head cases have recovered. We are certainly seeing war at its worst now. Many just bleed to death. I wish more of the people at home realised what war actually means, then they might do more to try to prevent it.

Notwithstanding these appalling experiences, in an early demonstration of the tenacity that was to characterise her stay in Spain, she signed off with the message: 'I would not like to have missed this experience for anything, gruesome though it is. I have not felt homesick yet.'

Of all the horror Murray witnessed in Spain, it was an incident later in the conflict that was to seal her lifelong hatred of fascism and warfare. In November 1938, she was working in Portbou, north of Barcelona, when an unusually large intake of child patients arrived in the hospital, all with disfiguring injuries to their hands and faces. Writing to her sister Agnes, Murray related how Italian aeroplanes had dropped

pretty little cigarette boxes and chocolate boxes with hand bombs neatly packed inside. The poor little mites of children picking up what they took to be the long-desired chocolate and quickly opening them were suddenly left handless, their faces burned beyond recognition. Nothing could surely be more brutal. What a bloody awful war this has been.

A conflict initially waged through field methods mirroring those of the Great War now featured civilian aerial attacks with all their intrinsic, callous brutality. As Murray had witnessed, in Spain modern warfare was born.

Though embroiled in the world of medicine, Murray's time in Spain allowed her to develop her political interests and views. Like her brothers, she had a great deal of faith in the Soviet Union, writing of Muscovite policy on Spain that 'we trust her [the Soviet Union] to do what is best in the long run'. Diametrically opposed to Murray's belief in the Soviet Union was her sense that the British Labour Party's policy on Spain amounted to 'criminal' inaction. In early 1937, she wrote home 'When are the Labour leaders in Britain going to come to their senses and do something about saving Spain?', a question echoed in her subsequent letters from Spain.

Having been posted to Barcelona in the first half of 1937, Murray had a first hand view of the internecine squabbles among republicans that were to rock that city in May 1937:

> The political situation in Catalonia is very complicated. There are so many different parties, and until one had actually lived in the district, it is very difficult knowing just who is who.

Prior to the civil war inside a civil war that broke out in Barcelona, Murray was moved back to the Huesca region, to a hospital at Poleniño, where she continued to treat both republican and nationalist patients, the latter of whom were surprised by the care they received, as she wrote to her brother Tom:

> We have dealt with many hundreds of seriously wounded men, and incidentally a dozen or more of them were fascists who were delighted with the treatment received in our hospital, and want to join the government side.

Conditions at Poleniño, largely through better organisation and increased government and foreign aid, were a huge improvement on those at Grañen. Murray and her co-workers were able to turn a private house

into an almost model hospital with sinks and basins of running water near the theatre – cold water only but such an advantage over Grañen with no running water at all. We have managed to make a very nice operating theatre which is praised by all who see it.

Such medical improvements, coupled with her political faith, left Annie Murray with an unshakeable faith in

Annie Murray with an ambulance lorry, many of which were purchased following the efforts of the British aid movement.

republican victory that lasted almost until the end of the conflict. Even after the March 1938 capitulation in Aragon she remained convinced of government triumph, remarking, 'Spain, I think, is going to go right forward now to victory after a short spell of setbacks.'

This resilience could not mask the fatigue that came with extended spells in Spain without leave and the hopelessness generated by not knowing just how long the war would last:

I wish things would get a move on. We expected to be out here for three or four months and we have been here now seven and there is little sign of a stoppage yet.

It is a tribute to Murray's dedication that at the conclusion of her first leave period for 14 months, in September 1938, she returned straight to the front, abstaining from the home comforts of Scotland for a life at war once again.

After a year in Spain, Annie Murray was moved again, this time south-west, to Huete, where she was appointed head nurse and put in charge of training new recruits. Happily, her wounded brother George was able to obtain a transfer there from a hospital in Murcia. He immediately wrote home boasting of her status as 'a favourite with patients and staff', and mentioning her fluent Spanish.

Through 1937, Murray felt increasingly that the nationalist air force was specifically targeting hospitals, sometimes successfully; a fellow nurse had lost an arm in a raid on a nearby American hospital. A further worry was the state of hospital equipment and Murray frequently dispatched missives home to press the British Medical Aid Committee into sending surgical instruments and medical clothing. Within this atmosphere of hardship grew a sense of camaraderie. Perceiving the importance of morale, Murray organised activities for patients and staff, such as 1937's Christmas Day fiesta, reported on here in a letter to Tom Murray:

I made with help a large Christmas pudding enough for 200 people, and it lasted for two days. It took four men to lift it into the pot. I went down to Murcia to buy such things as nuts, raisins, fruits etc. for the dinner, then spent the evening preparing the fruit. We had a concert in the afternoon, the dinner at 6 o'clock and a dance at night. It was a very enjoyable function. The young Spanish lads and girls are very good, natural actors, and they worked hard for this.

In April 1938, Nurse Murray was transferred to Barcelona again. She journeyed across Spain on a medical train which frequently came under nationalist fire. She admitted that republican morale was low but sought comfort in her political faith, writing that 'Russia had the same struggle before it was victorious.' In Barcelona, Murray worked for a Spanish surgeon and his team, though remained 'very anxious to get to the front again as I like it there better than anywhere else.'

Her wish was soon granted; from late May 1938, she found herself working on a hospital train, marginally behind the front line of engagement. During the Ebro campaign, the three Murrays were often within metres of a frontier reunion. However, though she treated many of their comrades, Annie was unable to meet directly with her brothers, writing, 'it is tantalising to think that we are so near each other and yet cannot meet'.

After an intensive time on the hospital train, where staff worked 24-hour shifts, Annie Murray was finally granted that long-overdue period of leave. She reflected upon her time at the Ebro in a letter to George and Tom:

By my experiences I have more idea of something of what you boys must have come through. As you say it is a wonder any human being is normal again after the dreadful things he has to come through in a war and especially such an offensive as that one you have seen.

On her return from leave, Murray found herself glad to be back in a country whose people she had fallen in love with regardless of its bloody war. In November 1938, she commented to Tom:

I feel very glad to be back here again; the people are so bright and optimistic, it doesn't seem to get one down like the continued moaning of most British people. They are a lovely and most kind-hearted race. I could stay here always.

Annie Murray's optimistic mood on her return was to be short-lived. As 1939 began, nationalist victory seemed increasingly inevitable, and in February she began the journey north from Barcelona towards France. On the way, she treated the walking wounded and volunteered to work in a refugee camp. She described the horror and destitution of the people she saw on that final journey:

I never want to see anything like it again. Hell is putting it mildly. This has left a black mark in my memory which I shall *never* be able to throw off.

Her last act of the Spanish war was to locate a friend of the Murray family,

Margaret Powell, who had been working in Spain, and obtain her release from a concentration camp near Perpignan. Murray then flew to Toulouse and took a ferry back to Britain, arriving alone and unheralded in London Victoria station, the silent and unassuming Scottish heroine of a titanic battle. 'It was,' she later said, 'the most important thing of my life. It was a terrific experience I would never like to have missed. I have certainly no regrets at having gone there at all.'[20]

PART 2
Scotland's War

CHAPTER 8
The Home Front:
Scottish Aid for Republican Spain

*I would say that there's never been the like of it in this country. I cannae
think of any village or town in the country where there were not masses
of people who were involved in raising money for Spain.*
James Miller, Methilhill

WHEN CIVIL WAR erupted in Spain, Scotland rallied to the republican cause with
remarkable speed and commitment. Initially, money and food were collected
by individuals, forming an unofficial humanitarian response that was to be
gradually succeeded by more formal and sustained campaigns. Reaction to
Spain's plight was immediate, instinctive and characterised by a generosity
above and beyond the call of duty and the reality of means available.

Concerts, fiestas and film showings were staged to raise both funds and
awareness, and 'Flag Days' for Spain became a regular feature of Scottish
life. Such was the scale of the aid Spain movement in Scotland, on 8 April
1937, CPGB leader Harry Pollitt felt able to declare in the *Daily Worker* that
'Scotland does better than any other part of the country in its contribution to
our fund.'

A large proportion of aid for Spain work was carried out by working class
women. Prams were utilised for collecting food from door-to-door, tins rattled
on street corners, and fundraising events were meticulously and prolifically
organised. Women, previously excluded from the male world of party politics
and trade unionism, became impassioned and emboldened supporters of
republican Spain, the volunteers of the home front.

Their work was complemented by that of a woman far more familiar with
the political sphere. The Duchess of Atholl was Conservative MP for Kinross
and West Perth, and the first Scotswoman to be elected to the Commons. From
the instant civil war started in Spain, she campaigned fervidly for the rights of
the elected republican government and its citizens, incurring the wrath of her
largely pro-Franco Conservative peers. Indeed, her support for the republic
more or less ended her political career.

The Duchess became chair of both the National Joint Committee for Spanish
Relief (formed in November 1936) and the Basque Children's Committee.
She toured Scotland on numerous occasions to muster support and funds for

SPANISH REFUGEE CHILDREN.

Edinburgh and District Joint Committee for Spanish Relief

Office:
c/o The Scottish Peace Council,
85 Hanover Street, Edinburgh, 2.
Phone 26573.

GREAT TWO DAYS

Spanish Fiesta and Fair

11.30 a.m. — 9 p.m. Daily

TO BE HELD IN

CENTRAL HALLS, TOLLCROSS, EDINBURGH

On Friday, 16th December, at 11.30 a.m.

TO BE OPENED BY

HIS EXCELLENCY

DON PABLO DE AZCARATE

Spanish Ambassador, London.

HER GRACE

THE DUCHESS OF ATHOLL
WILL PRESIDE.

On Saturday, 17th December, at 11.30 a.m.

TO BE OPENED BY

Mr NEIL BEATON

Chairman, Scottish Co-operative Wholesale Society

LADY WHITSON will preside

OUR AIM

To Raise at least £1000 to succour 10,000 Children.

3,700,000 Spanish Children, 337,000 of whom are under one year of age, are actually suffering from starvation at this very moment and are facing famine conditions. Thousands will die this winter unless immediate relief is provided. Lives can be saved for the meagre sum of 2/- per child per month.

We must succeed in our aim—to fail would mean disease and death to little children. We shall succeed with YOUR help.

Please help by sending a contribution in cash or in kind to any of the Receivers of contributions.

Bring and Buy!

[OVER

Publicity material for a two-day fundraising fiesta and fair organised by the Edinburgh and District Emergency Committee for Spanish relief.

the cause, stirring audiences into action with her oratory. In a meeting at St Andrew's Hall, Glasgow, on 18 January 1939, the Duchess showed that in spite of mounting republican setbacks and the effects of two and a half years of campaigning, she remained tireless in pursuit of her enemies and aims:

> Franco's victory in Spain means Hitler all over Europe. Franco claims to have two million people in lists who have committed 'political crimes' and if he wins they will be sent to concentration camps.

While the Duchess retained many conservative views – in her autobiography she stated that she supported republican Spain for the protection of British interests – neither her commitment to the cause of Scottish aid nor her political prescience can be doubted.

To coordinate fundraising efforts, from August 1936 joint aid boards were established in cities, towns and even villages across Scotland under the banner of Atholl's National Joint Committee for Spanish Relief. By mid-1937, Glasgow alone had 15 such groups. Though political hostilities often made harmony between different committees difficult, a unified Scottish Joint Committee for Spanish Relief was eventually established in February 1938. In May Edinburgh and Glasgow campaigners brought about an alliance of their respective trades councils to fight under the banner of 'Arms for Spain', reflecting a definite shift in the campaign movement towards demanding military aid alongside humanitarian. On the 15th of that same month, a 'broad church' group, including the Duchess of Atholl, Labour MP Wilfred Roberts and communist British Battalion Commander Fred Copeman, held a rally in Glasgow to demand for republican Spain the right to buy weapons.

Yet the progress of such joint campaigns continued to be checked by members of the Labour Party and STUC hierarchy who were irrevocably opposed to working with communists or members of the ILP, as the CPGB found when it instigated a campaign to engender solidarity.

The Unity Campaign was announced in the pages of the *Daily Worker* over

Collecting for Spain on a 'Flag Day' in Aberdeen, 1937. Such events were held several times a year in cities, towns and villages across Scotland for the duration of the Spanish Civil War.

the festive period of 1936. From the beginning of the fighting in Spain, the *Worker* had been a focal point for republican fundraising. In the first week of December 1936 alone, reader contributions amounted to £1,700, with a healthy sum from Scotland included in that total. Donating to the *Worker*'s appeal, a couple from Edinburgh wrote in with an accompanying note that hinted at the impoverished context in which so many Scots offered what aid they could: 'Please accept from man and wife the sum of one shilling towards Spanish workers. Sorry we can't send more. The reason is not hard to explain.'

The Unity Campaign was a joint venture between the CPGB, the ILP and the Socialist League wing of the Labour Party; it was founded, according to its manifesto, to demand 'unity of all sections of the working class against fascist reaction, war and the National Government.' Groups striving to help republican Spain would now, it was held, work together. There was considerable support in Scotland for the Campaign, and a number of large meetings were staged, culminating in a gathering at St Andrew's Hall in September 1937, when 3,000 people listened to speeches by Stafford Cripps, the group's figurehead, and International Brigader George Aitken.

On 3 February 1937, the *Glasgow Herald* labelled the Unity Campaign a 'grouping of extremists who pose a threat to democracy', while the Labour Party leadership denounced it from its inception, refusing to work with any movement containing CPGB members. Without their key support, and after splits with the ILP, the Unity Campaign struggled to make a tangible impact and gradually fizzled out.

While national movements proved difficult to build, galvanising local activity was more straightforward. The Scottish aid campaign for republican Spain largely revolved around activities in Glasgow and the surrounding areas. May Day 1937 can be taken as a yardstick indicating how entrenched support was there for the Spanish republic. It was the largest May Day rally since 1926, the year of the General Strike; 15,000 people turned out to march in endorsement of the day's main theme, 'Solidarity with Spain'. Of three resolutions passed at the conclusion of the rally, two were in support of republican Spain. The attendees roared with approval as the second resolution, sending 'Greetings to the comrades of all countries fighting in the International Brigades for the restoration of democracy', was read out.

The mood was summed up by a teenager from Paisley, who wrote in to the *Daily Worker* with a donation of 1s. 6d., his pocket money, and a demand to be allowed to fight in Spain where he promised to 'dust the pants off every fascist that comes my way'. Indeed, pocket money was regularly diverted to the Spanish cause by local youths, as a retailer from Bellshill confirmed in a March 1937 edition of the *Worker*:

Edinburgh Spain Emergency Committee

SPAIN is NOT Defeated

BUT

SPAIN'S DANGER IS OURS

ACT FOR SPAIN.   *ACT FOR BRITAIN.*

SAVE PEACE.

DEMAND ARMS and FOOD for SPAIN

Protect British Ships and British Seamen

Parliament meets on TUESDAY
Make Your Voice Heard

Rally to the Mound,
MONDAY FIRST, 30th January
At 10 p.m.

MANY PROMINENT AND REPRESENTATIVE SPEAKERS

Preliminary Notice—

G. R. STRAUSS, M.P.
KINGSLEY MARTIN (New Statesman)
G. J. MITCHELL, Advocate, and others,

speak on

"THE CRISIS"

On FRIDAY FIRST, 3rd February, at 7.30 p.m.

In the MUSIC HALL, George Street.

Reserved Seats—3d   **Unreserved—Collection**

BISHOP & SONS, LTD., PRINTERS, EDINR.

An Edinburgh Spain Emergency Committee poster from 1939. While campaigns earlier on in the war focused on humanitarian aid alone, a military element was added in later appeals, as is the case here.

ADMISSION VOUCHER

A Spanish Birthday Party

(TEA WITH A HOST OR HOSTESS)

Saturday, 3rd June 1939, from 5 to 8 p.m.

MUSIC HALL, GEORGE STREET, EDINBURGH

DON PABLO DE AZCARATE
(Late Spanish Ambassador, London), and
HER GRACE
THE DUCHESS OF ATHOLL,
D.B.E., D.C.L.

Will relate Recent Experiences and tell story of the
plight of Spanish Refugees still in France.

James A. Scott, Esq., M.A. (Rector, Trinity Academy), and Mrs Helen M. Scott
will be Chief Host and Hostess.

MUSICAL PROGRAMME ARRANGED BY DR. MARY GRIERSON

[P.T.O.

The genteel Edinburgh of 'tea hosts' was a far cry from the grassroots,
wall-advertised whist drives of Fife.

A girl, aged 7 years, came into our bookshop last week, put a halfpenny on the counter and asked for one of our weekly guarantor cards as she was keeping her halfpennies to help the Spanish children. Another little girl came with her at the end of the week and handed over 1d. This little girl is not only going to save her pennies, but is organising among her little playmates to contribute to the support of the Spanish people.

Another group who found young people willing to donate to the cause were the Glasgow Clarion Scouts. They organised a cycle relay to Barcelona, collecting money on their way through Scotland and England. Glaswegian cyclist Jack Shields remarked at the time: 'It is an inspiration to see how ready the young people of this country are to respond to the appeal of Spain.'

Not all fundraising required physical exertion. Cinema and theatre were used to highlight the Spanish republican cause and raise relief money. In February 1937, Maryhill Labour Club screened a film entitled *The Defence of Madrid* in front of a 500-strong audience. It was to set the tone for future broadcasts, as crowds flocked to see films like *The International Column*, *They Shall Not Pass*, and *Behind the Spanish Lines*, which were later shown to similar effect across Scotland.

The Scottish People's Film Association broadcast comparable films, raising £66 for aid over the summer of 1937. Glasgow Workers' Theatre Group also sought to raise both the profile of the cause and funds, performing on stage and street. Their adaptation of Jack Lindsay's *On Guard for Spain* was particularly successful, and toured nationwide.

Indeed, the arts provided a constant source of fundraising. Paul Robeson's performance in Glasgow was just one of many evenings organised to raise money through entertainment. Concerts typically involved a range of cabaret acts: the line-up for one such event, at Dixon Halls, Cathcart Road on 13 November 1938, included a choir, called the Greyfriars Quartet, soloist David Markson, Willie McLeod (a 'wonder boy pianist', according to the event's poster), 'Curious Comedy Couple' Herman and Grant, and the Simpson Ray Girls, a 'Talented Group of Child Dancers and Impersonators'.

While that particular event was organised by the Spanish Medical Relief Committee specifically, other fundraising drives saw city-wide cooperation. On 13 December 1936, six lorries, filled with foodstuffs and medical equipment, left George Square headed for Spain. The convoy's haul was collected after the Youth Foodship for Spain Committee had organised an appeal across Glaswegian aid groups. It was the first of many, proof that, on a local basis at least, different committees could work in unison.

Further emphasising the spirit of solidarity, a second Spanish Market for the benefit of the SAU was held in October 1937, as a joint venture with the Basque Children's Committee. Items made by Madrid women, such as fans, Toledo brooches and castanets, were sold to the Glasgow public and Spanish films screened. Day-to-day fundraising energies were focused on an Aid Spain shop at 11 Union Street, Glasgow. Opened by Hollywood star Raymond Massey, the shop was a receiving centre for donations of money, food, milk and medical supplies, as well as cash donations.

Political meetings on the subject of Spain became commonplace in Glasgow. As a happy side-effect they acted as fundraisers, with buckets passed around for donations. In terms of attendance, the meetings were an overwhelming success; it seemed Glaswegians had become as fanatical about the Spanish republic as they were about Celtic and Rangers. Perhaps the apex of this came in 1938, when simultaneous gatherings filled the City and St Andrew's Halls. Afterwards, both audiences marched on to the German consulate in protest at Nazi involvement in Spain. In Glasgow, the militant spirit of the NUWM, which was in itself active inside the Spanish aid movement, lived on throughout the civil war.

Assistance for the republican effort in Spain did not just take the form of fundraising and campaigning. A broad solidarity movement grew, with many supplementing their theoretical and financial support by putting their skills into practice. The *Glasgow Herald* reported an example of this on 20 May 1938:

It was authoritatively stated in Glasgow yesterday that numerous

INTERNATIONAL BRIGADE

Edinburgh and District Ex-Members' Association.

Hon. Treasurer—JOHN P. C. DUNLOP,

9 East Fettes Avenue, Edinburgh, 4.   'Phone 20754.

Office and Central Food Depot:

c/o DOTT, 8 Grosvenor Crescent, Edinburgh, 12.

The I.B.

FOOD CONVOY FOR SPAIN

Will arrive in Edinburgh, on Saturday, 21st January.

The Mound, 4 p.m.; Foot of Leith Walk, 4.30 p.m.

Donations, in Cash, for I.B. Disabled Ex-Members, Widows
and Orphans Fund, and Non-Perishable Food (Chocolate,
Sugar, Rice and Tinned Milk, Meat, Beans, Peas, Fish, Butter,
etc.), for Spain **urgently** required, and should be sent to above
Depot or brought to Meeting.

GREAT "AID SPAIN" RALLY

On SATURDAY, 21st JANUARY, at 7.30 p.m.

In the MUSIC HALL, GEORGE STREET.

Chairman—Rev. D. GORDON LIVINGSTONE, M.A.

Speakers:—Major **SAM WILD**, Battalion Commander;

Commissar **BOB COONEY**; Sir **ROBERT GREIG**;

W. P. EARSMAN, and other Members of the Convoy.

Musical Programme.   Come and Bring Your Friends.

Pay tribute to heroic Spanish People and International Brigade.

Admission—By Chocolate or Tin of Milk.

WARWICK & SONS LTD., EDINBURGH.

A 1939 Edinburgh and District International Brigade Ex-members Association flyer. Brigaders
such as Bob Cooney spoke of their experiences in Spain to raise the profile of aid appeals.
Note the novel approach to the admission 'fee'.

groups of engineers whose sympathies lie with the Spanish government are working in their spare time in various parts of the city to provide materials for the use of government forces in Spain.

The article went on to assert that garages had been re-equipped to convert old cars into ambulances and motorbikes into dispatch vehicles, as well as construct mobile washing machines for soldiers on the front lines. This was yet another example of Glasgow's wholehearted commitment to the cause. At times, it seems, the people of the city felt that they could single-handedly save Spain from Franco.

Though Edinburgh's aid movement was never on the scale of that in the west, the capital did make a significant contribution. The *Daily Worker* diligently reported some of the early individual contributions made, noting on 7 December, 'Over £20 and two wedding rings were collected at a meeting in the Oddfellows Hall.' On the 11th it reported that 'Eight members of the Granton Young Communist League borrowed a barrow from the manager of the local Co-operative and collected 1 cwt. of food.'

More officially, the aid movement in Scotland's capital emanated from the Edinburgh and District Joint Committee for Spanish Relief. As Chairman of the group, Brigader Tom Murray's wife Janet worked industriously to appeal to local people, organising and speaking at meetings and fundraising events such as December 1938's Spanish Fiesta and Fair at Central Halls, establishing a Spain Shop on Leith Street, and plying local newspapers with letters pleading for assistance. Perhaps inspired by the work of her sister-in-law Annie Murray, Janet was particularly involved with gathering medical aid for Spain. She wrote to the *Evening Dispatch* outlining the guiding principles and work of her group and praising the spirit of support they had benefited from:

> [our] principal object at the moment is the collecting of drugs, instruments and bandages, from doctors, chemists and others. We gladly mention the generous cooperation we are receiving from the BMA and the Pharmaceutical Society. Wholesale firms help us in the task of collecting from shops and individuals. In a country where major operations frequently have to be performed without anaesthetics, the need for these supplies requires no further emphasis. May I say for the benefit of those with political scruples that in medicine and nursing the only criteria of service are suffering and need.

Fundraising efforts in Edinburgh occasionally took a more genteel form than those in neighbouring areas like Glasgow; when the Edinburgh Basque Children's Committee was formed in June 1937, it hosted a garden fete for the local great and good at the home of Lady Salvesen. This was in contrast too to the wholly grassroots aid movement that arose in Fife. As an example of the difference in campaign types, advertising methods perhaps speak loudest. Where well-resourced groups in Edinburgh put out a constant stream of neatly-printed leaflets and had access to the press, in Fife the main source of advertising meetings and sloganeering was through whitewash on walls and bridges. Local pipe bands were deployed to generate support too, summoning people from their homes to donate dole money and tinned foods, and giving a send off to International Brigade volunteers at Lochgelly station. Whatever the method of garnering support, it certainly worked: for the duration of the war in Spain, Fifers donated with a munificence belying the poverty of a mining area suffering the very worst effects of economic depression.

Pivotal in this were the CPGB, who ensured that speakers and volunteers were on hand to corral the local population and receive their donations not only to republican Spain, but also in support of the families of local volunteers to the British Battalion. Within the CPGB ranks, a popular local figure and NUWM man, Bob Selkirk, was key in coordinating local efforts. Selkirk had become a town councillor in Cowdenbeath in 1935 and later became the first CPGB figure in Britain to be made a Freeman of the Burgh, perhaps offering some insight into the political context of 1930s Fife. While Selkirk was a regular keynote speaker at meetings alongside local Communist MP Willie Gallacher, he did not shy away from tramping the streets bearing a homemade megaphone, calling for his cart to be filled with food donations.

Also involved in the organisation of proceedings locally was the female-run East Fife Spanish Aid Committee and the regionally-strong Co-operative movement. Members of the Young Co-operators in Buckhaven did especially well in acquiring trucks from Co-operative Boards of Management to collect food from nearby mine villages, while in Bowhill, which was one of those very villages, a group of Co-operative mining families formed a Spanish aid committee. Co-operative clubs in Cowdenbeath and elsewhere were the scene of fundraising whist drives, which became large, community events.

Efforts in Fife were not restricted to larger settlements. Tiny villages gave generously at concerts and door-to-door collections. In Lumphinnans, methods of raising money did occasionally require the turning of a blind eye, as Rab Smith, then a child in the village, explained:

I remember at that time we sold a cigarette called 'Smoke Clouds'. We sold them in order to raise money to send to the Spanish aid fund. I'm sure they injured the health of the people that smoked them, because they had a terrible smell! Nevertheless, I wasn't concerned. I was concerned about saving Britain and saving the people in Spain.[21]

The belief contained in Smith's words – that saving Spain would in turn save Britain from fascist invasion – was shared not only by would-be volunteers to the International Brigades, but also by those active in the aid Spain movement across Fife and wider Scotland. Indeed, one of the slogans regularly daubed on Fife walls was 'Save Spain, Save Britain'. As another Fife campaigner, James Miller, asserted: 'We were acutely aware that if we lost the battle for Spain, then a world war was more than likely.'[22] With this in mind, the locals rallied to the cause with a remarkable generosity, and donated more food and money than many areas of greater population and prosperity.

In Aberdeen, the local NUWM spearheaded extremely successful fundraising efforts, while Dundee, a city which produced up to 123 volunteers to the British Battalion, the Trades and Labour Council was at the forefront of the local campaign for republican Spain, organising a Flag Day for the SAU in September 1936 and further events and appeals throughout the rest of the war.[23] Public meetings attracted remarkable crowds: 3,000 people turned out to hear 'back from the dead' Brigader David MacKenzie speak at Caird Hall in February 1937. By May 1937, Dundonians had raised enough money to buy and send an ambulance to Spain, and their vehicle arrived there on the 5th of that month. In late 1937, when a Spanish and Chinese Medical Aid and Food Depot on Reform Street was opened, the store was inundated with tins of milk, beans, peas, cocoa, herring, salmon and a wave of cash donations.

Dundee's Spanish Medical Aid Committee was prodigiously active, gathering medicines, medical instruments and food from local businesses for dispatch to Bilbao and other afflicted areas. There was, too, institutional support for aid appeals, and in January 1939 the City Council agreed to annul debts owed to them by the Spanish Aid Committee for the rental of shop units.

Perhaps the most significant Dundonian act of solidarity with republican Spain occurred as a reaction to the April 1937 nationalist bombing of Guernica. In May, the Dundee Spanish Aid Committee discussed the possibility of establishing a 'colony' for Basque refugee children, an idea that had already been raised in west Fife, where the villagers of Lumphinnans, Lochore, Glencraig and Bowhill realised that they would be unable to summon resources to make it a reality. The task of planning the provision of a safe haven therefore fell to Dundee.

Once the idea of a children's home had been mooted, labour organisations in Dundee were quick to pledge their support. In early June, the local Trades and Labour Council endorsed the establishment of a Basque Children's Fund. Bodies as diverse as the Bakers' Union, the Blind Institution, the Dundee Breakfast Club and the Women's Liberal Association donated generously. Dockers took on a team of locally-berthed Spanish seamen at football and

Basque children at the Montrose home. Despite the wary looks on their faces, the children thrived in their Scottish setting.

raised a hefty sum on the gate and from donations, while the Dundee School of Music staged a concert in Caird Hall. By the end of the month, 34 different groups were on board.

In July, a Basque Children's Committee was launched to search for suitable premises in which to house children, nearly 4,000 of whom had been evacuated to southern England, where they were now residing in temporary accommodation. Various sites in Dundee were considered, only to be deemed unfit or unavailable, but suitable premises were found 30 miles up the coast in Montrose: Mall Park, owned by the Dundee Free Breakfast Mission, had room for 25 children. When the first residents arrived in late September 1937, a local councillor, Bailie McGregor, protested; citing alleged disorder caused by migrant Basques elsewhere in Britain, his was a rare voice of dissent.

The children stepped off their train at Montrose to a welcome spelled out on a banner. They integrated well into the community and donations towards maintaining the home continued to pour in for the duration of their stay, which came to an end in the summer of 1938. In November 1937, at a packed public meeting at Caird Hall staged in solidarity with the Basque children, the young refugees provided the entertainment, and an exhibition of their drawings was held at Dundee Training College later that month. Though distraught with homesickness and worry for their families in Spain, the children did find great contentment in Scotland's only Basque refugee colony, and two, Encarnacion and Esther Benavente, remained in the country long after their fellow refugees had departed. Bene Gonzalez, 15 years old on the day she arrived at Mall Park, recalled in 1985 that the children had lived 'immensely happily, and joyfully'. [24] Undoubtedly, Scotland had left its mark on the young Basques, but so too had they affected the people of Dundee and Montrose: rarely before had a cause been embraced by communists, socialists, liberals, churches and businesses as theirs was.

Another example of less conventional aid comes from the Borders town of Hawick. In December 1936, activists from the local NUWM took over a disused woollen mill on Mansfield Road and announced their intention to provide clothing for republican forces in Spain by re-opening the plant as a co-operative, a project which had been proposed two months earlier by Hawick's only CPGB councillor, Willie Stoddart. Though support in the traditionally Conservative town was far from guaranteed (in the following months, at the annual dinner of the Callants' Club, General Franco received praise for being the saviour of 'Christian civilisation'), there were enough local pro-republicans to provide a workforce. The mill was refurbished and production commenced in January 1937.

Though initially subsidised by a nationwide funding campaign, the mill soon became self-sufficient as private orders were taken on to subsidise the making of gloves, hats and scarves for Spanish republican fighters. David MacKenzie made a speech in Hawick announcing that the town was 'now known not only throughout Britain, but also throughout Spain as the place where the workers have given material evidence of their support for the fight against fascism'. Through 1937 and into 1938, the Hawick Workers' Mill, as it became known, successfully pulled off the twin accomplishments of offering practical assistance to the Spanish republic, and employing a 20-strong workforce in a small town devastated by unemployment. However, the Workers' Mill could not escape the economic climate of Britain in 1939 and, as the republican cause in Spain melted in defeat, local mills sought to win contracts in the newly-lucrative war preparation market. It had for a time, though, been a remarkably successful venture: a New Lanark for the highly-politicised Scotland of the 1930s.

Scotland's largest single contribution to the campaign for Spanish aid

A Food Ship For Spain wagon in Aberdeen, typical of those seen across Scotland. Generous donations facilitated the sending of a vessel from Glasgow on 18 December 1938.

British aid – including corned beef – is gratefully received in Madrid.

was not focused on one particular geographical area, although the Glasgow Trades Council played an instrumental role. The sending of a food ship to Spain was first proposed at a December 1937 meeting between Edinburgh and Glasgow Trades Councils. Over the subsequent six months, an appeal to raise £10,000 for the venture received significant backing throughout the country. In the summer of 1938, a shop was opened in Dundas Street, Glasgow, for the donation of 'canned foods for the magnificent people of Spain.'

On 18 December, Captain McCrady and his crew set out from the Broomielaw destined for Spain with a 1,000 ton cargo of foodstuffs on board. Despite sailing through militarily dangerous waters for no pay, the crew arrived speedily, and was able to start distributing the ship's wares to starving, under siege Spaniards in late 1938. Buoyed by the success of this endeavour, the Trades Councils proposed sending a second ship, though this was never to materialise owing to an intensification of the blockade on Spanish waters. The food ship was a rare example of inter-city working in Scottish aid operations, but in many ways, that cooperation had come too late.

By March 1939, republican defeat appeared unavoidable, and the aid movement in Scotland and elsewhere switched its focus to the plight of Spanish refugees. Half a million people had fled or been evacuated from former republican territory in northern Spain, most hoping to escape nationalist reprisals by settling in France. When they arrived on the northern side of the Pyrenees, they were instead placed in concentration camps.

Offers from individual households to give shelter to refugees in Scotland flooded in. The Co-operative Society in Rothesay was able to provide accommodation for 200 children in its holiday camp there and a Clyde-built ship, the SS *Sinaia*, was chartered by the National Joint Committee for Spanish relief and a British Committee for Refugees from Spain to transport 1,800 exiles from France to a new life in Mexico. Scottish aid committees were quick to commit the money to pay for the conveyance of 20 men and their families on the *Sinaia*, and the Glasgow and District Joint Committee for Spanish Relief held a fundraising fiesta, which raised £1,400.

The newly-formed International Brigade Association (IBA), with George Murray at its helm in Scotland, soon took over the mantle of campaigning for the rights of exiled republicans and all of those who fought in Spain. The IBA was to continue its work for the duration of the Franco era, agitating against British collaboration with his regime (not least in 1947, when the Labour government signed an economic treaty with Spain). The IBA also brought into the open the atrocities being perpetrated on imprisoned republicans in Spain and offered support to wounded ex-International Brigaders.

Whatever the period of struggle against Franco's nationalists, in villages, towns and cities, as individuals or in organisations, Scots, and particularly

Scotswomen, built a solidarity movement of real consequence and clout. They gave when it seemed they had so little left to give, materially and emotionally, as James Miller acknowledged:

> We did our best, and we must congratulate our working class women on a tremendous effort – the thousands and thousands of pounds, the shoes, the clothes that were gathered and sent to Spain, and the food of all kinds. I'm just proud to have been part of that.

CHAPTER 9

A Home Guard:
The Reaction of Relatives

Annie was in very good spirits and not a bit worried about going out
to the fighting zone. Of course, it is much worse for the people left
at home, isn't it?
Margaret Murray, Perthshire and London

THE AID MOVEMENT offered relatives of those who had gone to fight in Spain
an opportunity to embroil themselves in the same struggle as their kindred.
The experience of being a relative back in Scotland was often traumatic,
with news of the location and health of loved ones only sporadically filtering
through Spain's wartime postal service. Long periods without dispatches from
behind republican lines naturally sharpened anxiety. This was the experience
of Mrs L Lacey, the Glaswegian mother of 21-year-old volunteer George
Keegan, who had arrived in Spain for a second spell in spring 1937. With no
news of his whereabouts and exasperated by her efforts to wrest information
from the CPGB, she aired her concerns to Motherwell ILP representative David
Murray:

> What do you think can have become of him after his foolish escapade? I
> am very anxious about him. I do not know where to get any information
> and I should be sincerely grateful if you could give me any.

Murray managed to ascertain that Keegan had deserted, observing rather
disconcertingly that if he freely returned 'nothing at all might happen, as the
Spanish people are curiously lenient and exacting by turns'. Despite utilising
his connections in Spain, Murray was unable to locate the young volunteer,
and it was only when he was wounded at Quinto in late August that news of
his situation emerged. By September, Keegan was back in Scotland.

Brigader missives that did reach Scotland often encouraged relatives and
friends to involve themselves in the aid campaign. Eddie Brown wrote home
in May 1937 to press home the importance of assistance:

> We hope that you are doing as much for Spain as you possibly can, as
> help of all descriptions is needed badly. The more help you can give, the

easier the job for the International Brigades and the quicker international fascism will be smashed.

Attempts were sometimes made to strike political and geographical chords in the hope recipients of letters would be spurred into action. Thomas McWhirter wrote home ahead of a Glasgow-based fundraising event in February 1938:

We, Glasgow Boys, members of the glorious 15th Brigade, send revolutionary greetings from the battlefields of Spain. We are proud to be sons of Glasgow, carrying on her fighting traditions, and we sincerely hope tonight's great gathering will mark a new stage in the advance of the revolutionary movement.

The family of Annie, George and Tom Murray were energetic activists, although, given their political convictions, they needed no encouragement to stir them into action.

As Chairman of the Edinburgh and District Joint Committee for Spanish Relief, Janet Murray worked diligently for the aid for Spain movement. For six months of her tenure, she was without her Brigader husband, Tom. Though racked with loneliness in his absence, she understood and supported his decision to go to Spain. Writing to him in April 1938, she confessed:

I have never experienced such a feeling of complete desolation and I daren't give myself time to sit and think. Nevertheless I would not have it otherwise. I believe as sincerely as you in the course you have taken and in the rightness of your action.

Despite long gaps between replies, Janet wrote to her husband on alternate days, often exhibiting the kind of sentiments more frequently heard from soldiers on the front line. After republican successes in the summer of 1938, she wrote:

The fight is by no means over and we simply must get arms across to you soon. I would gladly give my life if only we could do something to get things going here.

For all her resolution and spirit, Janet Murray shared the concerns of all those Scottish families who had relatives fighting in Spain. Writing prior to the crossing of the River Ebro (see Chapter 14), she described the blindness that came with being so far away:

THESE SOLDIERS OF THE PEOPLE

GAVE

THEIR

LIVES

ROBERT BRIDGES   ROBERT MASON   ROBERT SAYER   WILLIAM JOHN DICKSON

TO SAVE THE HOMES OF SPAIN
TO SAVE OUR HOMES IN BRITAIN

HAROLD FRY   JOHN McLEOD ROSS

and

JAMES RUTHERFORD   JOHN GILMOUR   JOHN DAGLISH   SAMUEL WHITE   JOHN BERRY

A poster of fallen Scottish Brigaders. Back home, it was left to their relatives to pick up the pieces and continue the fight.

You are now having the test you talked of. I know that you will be acquitting yourself with credit. My imagination fails me when I try to think of what you are undergoing and the life you are living. I do hope things go well with you both [Tom and George]. As you can imagine, this is an anxious time for us at home here, but we are doing our best to keep from worrying too much.

In the following week, still having heard nothing from Spain, Janet described the experience of receiving word that eight Scots had been killed in fighting: 'My heart sank. I do hope nothing happens to you. The anxiety is terrible but I try to keep going.' One can only imagine the elation she felt on subsequently learning that Tom, George and Annie were well.

Janet Murray did not have to suffer her agony alone. Tom and his two siblings had left behind a further five sisters, Agnes, Lily, Margaret, Susan and Violet, who were all involved in campaigns for republican Spain. Two of the sisters had tried their utmost to serve there themselves.

Like so many supporters of the republic, Lily Murray bemoaned the foreign assistance received by the nationalists, and the intransigent non-interventionism of the British government, writing to Janet in January 1937, 'Things out in Spain are very grave indeed and this fresh push of Franco's with the aid of so many Germans and Italians must make it very hard for the government side to keep their end up.' The following month, she wrote:

> It almost frightens one to think of it all, and this ban on volunteers will just be like everything else – carried out strictly by Britain while Germans and Italians pour in. The British people will not have their sorrows to seek ere long.

Lily was centrally involved in fundraising for Spain in her home town of Perth. Like her brother and sister-in-law, she did not shy away from making speeches, in which she regularly quoted the Marxist political scientists whose works she had studiously read.

As a nurse, Violet Murray was keen to work in Spain, especially following the receipt of a telegram from Annie in early 1937, which simply read: 'Come out if possible. Work for you here.' Having registered her interest in volunteering with Harry Pollitt and the Spanish Aid Committee, Violet confessed to Janet Murray: 'I am all excited that I will be able to *do* something really worthwhile for my fellow comrades in need.' As with volunteers to the International Brigades, Violet's decision to try and go to Spain was influenced by anti-fascist struggles on the streets of Britain. In her adopted home city of London, she was deeply involved in local campaigns against the BUF, regularly taking part in demonstrations and counter-demonstrations. She described one such occasion:

> I went down to Bermondsey last Sunday, and I shall never forget the scenes I saw. I thought once or twice I should be arrested but was very fortunate in getting home with no bones broken. Heads cut and people being trampled on and awful things happening and the police were just hitting out *anywhere* and at anyone. It makes one all the more anxious to go to Spain when one sees what fascism is really doing at home.

By early October 1937, Violet's departure for Spain appeared to be imminent. However, CPGB officials decided that she was too valuable to the domestic struggles against fascism, and at the start of November the prospective volunteer received the disappointing news that she would not be allowed to go to Spain. Lily wrote consolingly: 'sorry to hear about Spain. Tom thinks you are doing better work here all the same.'

Agnes, Margaret and Susan Murray were, like Violet, card-carrying members of the CPGB. Susan, who worked as a hairdresser and read the *Daily Worker* between cuts, was involved in numerous anti-fascist demonstrations and street tussles with the BUF. In a letter to Tom, she described the confrontational political milieu:

> As I helped to carry stuff down to a house where the Hampstead Party keep banners, platforms and literature, about half a dozen fascists followed us and prowled about with intentions of breaking in, so I stayed all night.

Given the efforts of the Murray sisters, it is no surprise that Scottish campaigners came in for particular praise from Londoners, as Agnes remarked in a letter to Lily: 'In the Party itself the Scotch are looked upon with admiration and respect.' Agnes and Margaret, who were both nurses, busied themselves rallying support for their causes among colleagues and were keen fundraisers for the Spanish republic. Having a young daughter, Agnes was unable to take what otherwise would have been a straightforward decision to volunteer for service in Spain. However, with no maternal responsibilities, in July 1937 Margaret became the fifth Murray to enlist for service in Spain, informing Janet:

> I have applied to go out to nurse in Spain too, so I am just waiting till Dr Morgan of the Spanish Aid Committee returns, when a new unit is to be formed before I know definitely when I shall be going.

Nonetheless, after awaiting a call to duty for two months, Margaret announced that domestic affairs would in fact now prevent her from going to Spain; she had become engaged to be married. The Murray family, though, had already gone far beyond the call of duty. They, like so many left behind in Britain, had taken their relatives' fight on as their own, channelling their energies into positive action for republican Spain. Mothers, wives, sisters, brothers, sons and daughters had become soldiers of the home front.

CHAPTER 10

Scots for Franco:
The Friends of National Spain

Are there any young men from this country so foolish as to
interfere in this matter?
Frederick MacQuisten, Unionist MP for Argyllshire

THE PEOPLE OF Scotland were not uniformly pro-republican. Opponents of the government side in Spain fell into two camps: those who positively championed Franco, and those who opposed the republicans and therefore lent their support to the nationalists by default. Both factions were influenced in their views by republican atrocities against the Catholic Church.

In the former of those two groups was the influential *Catholic Herald and Glasgow Observer*. In a September 1936 report claiming that attacks on religious figures and buildings were undertaken entirely at the behest of Moscow, it went on to justify Franco's rebellion:

This war was not between the National Government and rebels, but a war between atheism, communism and syndicalism on the one hand, and the party which stood for law and order, nationality and religion [on the other].

In conveying its message, the newspaper was not above propaganda and even bare-faced lying: in December 1936, it reported that the republican government had created an entire battalion of prostitutes to defend Madrid. An enduring image, perhaps, but not a truthful one.

On 12 September 1936, the *Catholic Herald*'s reaction to the mobilisation of the pro-republican aid movement was to call for Catholics to denounce supporters of the Spanish republican government; it asserted that 12,000 Scottish Catholics had already signed up and that the 'Red Army' was intent on the 'banishment of religion from Spain.' In taunting language, it asked, 'Have you less courage than the slaves of materialism?' and demanded that readers 'declare that Christ is your King'. Supporters were then asked to sign and send in the following pledge:

I protest against the organised slaughter of Christians and the destruction of property in Spain by Communists who have by force usurped the place of the elected representatives of the Spanish people. I call upon His Majesty's Government to use its influence for the protection of the Spanish patriots who are fighting for civil and religious liberty against a Communistic dictatorship which is a threat to the peace and stability of the British Empire.

It was certainly a powerful statement to make, and powerful too was the provocative move of labelling the entire Popular Front government communist. In parallel with republican aid efforts, the newspaper launched its own Spanish Relief Fund for 'the victims of the anti-God campaign in Spain.' 'All over the country', the campaign's maiden advertisement proclaimed, 'money is being donated to the Spanish Reds. What are we going to do for the Catholic victims of hatred? Should our charity not exceed that of those who have no faith?'

In the same way that pro-republicans believed nationalist victory in Spain would mean the spread of fascism across Europe, those behind this appeal asserted that 'Unless the Church wins in Spain, it cannot survive long in this country'. In a somewhat unorthodox indemnity scheme, readers were then asked to 'Pay something as an insurance premium against a No-God attack in Scotland.'

Donations were made to the fund primarily by west coast residents often anonymously or under pseudonyms such as 'Lover of St Joseph' and 'Remember Alcazar'. Lacking the tidal wave of popular support that accompanied the republican fundraising movement, the *Catholic Herald*'s Relief Fund was never a serious rival for the pound notes and affections of the people of Scotland. It did send several donations of over £100 to religious organisations in Spain, but in truth only a small number of Catholics took up the invitation to 'show their practical sympathy with those who are the victims of the anti-God campaign'.

John McGovern, the MP for Shettleston. His tirades against the Catholic Church in Spain caused upset among some constituents.

Media opposition to pro-republican Scottish involvement in Spain appeared in the stories, editorials and letters pages of a number of other newspapers, and, as witnessed in the *Daily Mail*'s sensationalist coverage of the Jarama machine-gunner prisoners, sections of the press sought to undermine support for the Spanish republic through misreporting and embellishment. On 29 January 1938, the *Daily Express* claimed that 22 Scottish members of the British Battalion captured by nationalist forces at Teruel had been shot on Christmas Day because they had been forced by the republican authorities to adopt Spanish citizenship, making them liable to punishments usually reserved for natives. Furious denials of the story were issued by Harry Pollitt, and the scientist JBS Haldane, a staunch supporter of the Spanish republic, made a mockery of the *Express* article by confirming that he had enjoyed Christmas dinner with the men some 50 miles away from Teruel. There is no evidence of any International

This short book, published in 1938, consolidated in writing some of the BUF policies that had pushed many Scots to oppose fascism, whether in Scotland or Spain.

Brigader having been forced to take Spanish citizenship. In short, the story was a piece of mischief aimed at destabilising the republican movement in Scotland and beyond.

Scottish supporters of the Spanish republic did not take such press bias lightly. Trade union branches were quick to express their misgivings; as early as August 1936, the Kirkcaldy Branch of the National Union of Railwaymen passed a resolution stating that it viewed 'with apprehension the lies and slanders being circulated by the reactionary press'. Later, a Glasgow Newsagents' Emergency Committee organised a boycott against the *Sunday Mail* on account of its anti-republican bias, resulting in the unavailability of the newspaper in thousands of shops. The impact of negative press reports was felt in Spain, too, as one anonymous mother of a Brigader from Govan wrote to the *Daily Worker* in April 1937:

I just had a letter from my son. He seems quite happy and content and

A 1933 booklet in which Oswald Mosley set out his vision of a Fascist Britain. Propaganda pieces such as this helped the BUF push their ideas into the public domain, provoking demonstrations of support and an anti-fascist backlash.

wishes he could get at the press who are telling such foul lies about how they have been betrayed with his Maxim gun, and he would give them a fright.

Writing home in June 1937, volunteer Jimmy Moir communicated his own disgust at the press with the sarcastic comment:

It seems as if I am getting near the end of the last page [of the letter] and have written a great deal about nothing at all. When I get back home, I'll try for a job with the *Daily Mail* or *The Times*.

Anti-republican editorial content appeared in the pages of the *Glasgow Evening Times* and the *Glasgow Evening Citizen*. Not as rabidly pro-nationalist as the *Express* and the *Mail*, they appeared lukewarm to the idea of a Franco victory but were definitely hostile towards the republican side. In its editorials, the *Evening Times* portrayed the elected Spanish government as a puppet of the Soviet Union, averring on 15 July 1937 that Madrid and the republican government were under the control of the SIM, scathingly concluding:

Evidently the so-called Spanish government, which our Socialist friends constantly support, is quite unable even to control the police in Spain! Apparently its authority is not sufficient to save either its own partisans or foreign volunteers who went to its assistance, from being dropped into prison and shot! What sort of a government is that? It certainly cannot reasonably claim to be the Government of Spain.

ILP activist David Murray responded by slating the *Evening Times* as 'actually a fascist paper or near a fascist paper, one of the most reactionary in the district'. Meanwhile, despite protestations that 'Our readers know that we are not partisans of either Fascism or Communism', the *Evening Citizen* was even more transparently pro-Franco. In an editorial published on 21 September 1937, it labelled the republican government a 'junta' and expressed incredulity at the way in which General Franco had generally been described as a 'rebel', arguing that the nationalist government had attained legitimacy as 'General Franco governs more than half of Spain and the rest of that country is disunited and practically without a supreme government.' The inference was that nationalist rule had become the most viable option for Spain:

The continued pretence that the Junta in Valencia is the legitimate Spanish government, and that General Franco, who exercises all the functions of government over a vastly greater number of Spaniards, is little better than a bandit, is farcical... General Franco has obtained the support of a very large number of the Spanish people, and has given them orderly government and security.

The *Citizen's* anti-republican position found favour among some of its readers. 'After reading the anti-Franco balderdash purveyed by some newspapers and MPs', wrote a correspondent identified only as 'Saltire', 'it is a relief to turn to the sensible leading articles in the *Citizen'*. The pithily-nicknamed 'Gib' assented with the view that 'If Franco wins, peace will be established' and advocated the inauguration of a dictatorship. In a warning to pro-republicans, 'Gib' concluded, 'We will certainly make a mistake if we lead the Francoists to think we are against them and favouring their opponents.' In April 1938, a correspondent went even further, asserting that 'Franco and the Christians came to the rescue of Spain and civilisation.'

Such sentiments often came from Scottish Catholics. Their anti-republicanism had the side-effect of causing difficulties for a Labour Party that, particularly in Glasgow, relied heavily on their votes. While instinctively opposed to Franco's nationalists, Party officials realised that by outwardly backing the republic they ran the risk of alienating some Catholic voters, which contributed to Labour's slow, often cool support for the republican aid movement in Scotland.

David Murray's comments on the effects of this policy in the Motherwell district were applicable to all of Scotland. He wrote in an ILP bulletin that 'the local Labour Party has been very loath to disturb its possession of what is called the Roman Catholic vote', a theme he continued in a letter to Josiah Wedgwood MP:

> The Labour Party is afraid to tackle the question of Roman Catholic Church influence and is piling up a store of trouble for itself. In my own district, the obvious angling for the Catholic vote has distinctly alienated the people who owe no allegiance to that church, and who are not only more dependable but are also in the majority.

Another ILP man, John McGovern, MP for the heavily-Catholic area of Shettleston, bore the brunt of Glaswegian Roman Catholic hostility. McGovern, a Catholic himself, travelled to Spain early on in the war for an insight into the level of persecution suffered by the church at the hands of republicans. He returned convinced that the government had halted attacks on Catholic figures and property and released a pamphlet entitled *Why the Bishops Back Franco*, lambasting the church for its suppression of the Spanish poor and its collaboration with Franco. For his troubles, he received torrents of abuse during the mass meetings at which he spoke following the Spanish trip and there were heated debates between pro-republicans (often Catholic themselves) and those who took umbrage at his portrayal of their church.

Addressing a crowd of 2,500 at a Parkhead gathering in late 1936, McGovern opened with a defence of the right of Spaniards to take strike action over their disgust at the wealth of the Catholic Church:

> If you were tramway-men working for two pesetas or four pence per day, and came on strike to better your conditions and found that the buses and trams were owned by the Catholic Church, and the clergy in the pulpits were denouncing you as 'dupes of Moscow' for going on strike, what would you British working men do? You would denounce the clergy as the enemy of the people. That's what the workers in Spain did, and I for one don't blame them.

To cries of 'liar!' from some sections of the audience, McGovern spoke of a 16-year-old boy he had met in Spain who had been 'instructed' by a priest to join the nationalist uprising in return for work upon Franco's victory. Attracting further derision, he stated that 'the lumber industry, the iron industry, even dog-racing and bull-fighting' were owned by the Catholic church. Aware of the upset his words were causing his devotedly Catholic constituents, McGovern defiantly remarked: 'If I had a thousand seats, I would lose them on this issue; my self-respect is more important to me than any seat in the country.' He further incensed many of those present by informing them that the Catholic church in Scotland was collecting money to fund Franco's bombing of innocent women and children and described the local priest, Father Daniels, as 'an apostle of Christian terrorism'. A furious constituent barked at McGovern, 'Why do you go to Spain and come back and denounce the Church? Are you a Catholic? You are a turn-coat.' More tersely, another audience member apparently replied 'Sit on your arse, for God's sake.'

McGovern's Catholic opponents were no doubt influenced by the anti-republican warnings emanating from church leaders. In August 1936, the Ancient Order of Hibernians in Glasgow began a campaign condemning the Spanish government for allegedly organising state terror against priests and nuns, and the ransacking of religious buildings. Individual clergymen also railed against the republican regime. Archbishop MacDonald of St Andrews and Edinburgh lamented that persecuting the church in Spain meant persecuting Jesus Christ. In a pastoral letter, he described events in melodramatic language:

> The appalling outbreak of Communism in Spain has shocked the whole

civilised world. The unspeakable atrocities perpetrated against priests and nuns, the horrible outrages on sacred images, on churches, on the Eucharist itself, the insensate revolt against all law and order – these prove beyond doubt that Christianity is the enemy aimed at. God himself is the foe.

By implication, volunteering to serve in Spain or even contributing to aid appeals would not be an act in defence of democracy or war-afflicted civilians, but an attack on God. Such teachings did impact upon the views of some working class Catholics. John McNair, an influential ILP figure, wrote to David Murray in November 1936 informing him of some of the difficulties he had encountered whilst speaking on Spain:

I had three meetings in Fife which, the local comrades were good enough to tell me, were successful, but there was a strong Catholic opposition. I understand that [Willie] Gallacher's meetings in this constituency were broken up by the Catholics. While I was speaking I realised the force of the opposition and its effectiveness as it was led by a local priest, who was no fool, and the secretary of the Young Catholics' League.

Reporting support for Franco in working class areas in more acerbic tones, the February 1938 edition of Motherwell ILP's news bulletin vituperated:

De-classed degenerates in Craigneuk are stupid enough to chalk 'Up Franco' on the streets; lumps who never had a square meal in their lives. They are crazy but fascism draws its cannon fodder from such degenerates.

After complaints from readers about these remarks, the next issue contained a retraction, of sorts:

We do not for a moment infer that all the folks up in Craigneuk are of this type, nor do we allege that this district has any monopoly of what is termed the 'lumpen proletariat'. None the less, the debatable land between Motherwell and Wishaw is the only area where Franco slogans have been chalked above street announcements.

This political friction was a clear symptom of unrest among working class Catholics. Nevertheless, the influence of Catholicism in determining which side Scots took in the Spanish Civil War was relatively insignificant. This is borne out by the fact that so many Scottish volunteers to the International Brigade

STREETS BLOCKED BY ANTI-FASCISTS

111 ARRESTS IN DISORDERS DURING MOSLEY MARCH

STONES AND FIREWORKS THROWN AT POLICE

ROUTE DIVERTED AFTER OPPONENTS BUILD BARRICADES

Wild scenes in south-east London marked the n/ discussed march of the British Union of Fascists . Millbank to Bermondsey yesterday.

There wer were injured it

The wors Borough High in an effort to

So serious wi from these thore

Sir Philip directed arrange crowds which ga late in the even

In the scuffl Reinforcements had a hostile rec hurled at them.

There was their batons whi arrived with spe

TWO RIV

At the Londor assembly a stre was concentra speaker cars tenders, and bu Sir Oswald Mc suit over a blacl made a short marchers Chee ing marked the ression.

NUMBER 12, 1938.

WILD SCENE IN ABERDEEN

ANTI-FASCIST CROWD THROW MISSILES

FOUR PERSONS ARE INJURED

Four persons were hurt during in Torry, Aberdeen. section of

COURT DOOR SCENE

ANTI-FASCIST CROWD DEMONSTRATE

SEVEN ARRESTS MADE IN ABERDEEN CLASH

COMMUNISTS AND FASCISTS FIGURE IN WILD SCENE

POLICE GUARD VAN WHEN SECTION OF CROWD ATTEMPTS RUSH

MISSILES FLYING: BATONS DRAWN IN LODGE WALK SCUFFLE

Remarkable scenes were witnessed in Aberdeen last night

BATON PLAY AT ABERDEEN

Fascist Speakers Get Rowdy Reception at Open-Air Meeting

Aberdeen City Police had to draw their batons and force back a crowd of about 10,000 before the start of a Fascist demonstration in the Market Stance, Aberdeen.

While the crowd was being swept back, a young woman was bowled

of the Aberdeen branch of the Independent Labour Party, which had started previously, had to be temporarily stopped, although the party remained on the platform.

REARGUARD FORMED When the Fr van started out from

W K A J Chambers tioned a meeting at the crowd Attempts were lained by the police

which the van was addressed the crowd for shouting

rowd followed a number l to be drawn in a scuffle (...)

l been made to effect the re one detained, and there was approval when a speaker suf should return to the van unt

Newspaper headlines from the 1930s highlighting the surge of fascist activity in Aberdeen, and anti-fascist reaction.

came from Catholic backgrounds. The position of Scottish Catholic Brigaders was encapsulated in words written by a friend about James Cassidy, a Maryhill man killed at Jarama, published in the *Daily Worker* on 25 March 1937:

> While Cassidy was a Catholic, he did not believe the lies that the fight of the Government in Spain was against the church and religion. He recognised that the fight in Spain was an issue that concerned all lovers of democracy, and he had no hesitation in volunteering to fight.

Noteworthy political support for Franco in Scotland was similarly negligible. What backing there was came from the aristocracy and small BUF branches, most markedly in Cathcart. So infinitesimal were Scottish BUF numbers, though, the sending of a battalion to fight for Franco, as happened with Ireland's Blue Shirts, was unthinkable. As the experiences of Aberdeen and elsewhere showed, wherever the BUF materialised in Scotland, they were crushed by a far weightier anti-fascist movement.

Among the most solidly pro-Francoist group in Scotland were the aristocracy, in particular those with strong links to the armed forces. Prominent here was the 8th Earl of Glasgow, formerly an influential member of the British Navy and by the 1930s a devotee of Oswald Mosley. In common with other pronationalists, he consistently demanded belligerent rights for Franco, confessing in the House of Lords that he could not see 'why this country should insist on the withdrawal of Italian troops from Spain before they have finished the work they were sent for.' Colonel RG Dawson, of Orenill, Braco, berated the Duchess of Atholl, his local MP, for her pro-republican stance, circulating a pamphlet entitled *My Reply* that questioned the validity of Atholl's antipathy towards Franco.

Sympathy for this view came from Captain Archibald Maule Ramsay, the Conservative MP for Peebles. A rabid anti-semite, Ramsay viewed the Spanish Popular Front government as the centre of an international Jewish–Marxist conspiracy. He formed the United Christian Front, to fight 'to prove the real fact, that General Franco is fighting the cause of Christianity against the anti-Christ.' He received support from the Earl of Home, father of Lord Dunglass MP, acting parliamentary private secretary to Neville Chamberlain during the Munich peace agreement. From 1940, Ramsay, a member of the Council of the Nordic League, an 'association of race-conscious Britons', was interned for four years by the British government as a consequence of his political activities and beliefs. In parliament, Lord Marley alleged that Ramsay was Hitler's chosen Gauleiter for Scotland should Germany emerge victorious from World War Two. The Peebles MP's right-wing extremism was exceedingly rare in Scotland.

While Ramsay was arguably the most unequivocal individual advocate of Franco in Scotland, collective aristocratic support came from a group whose figurehead was directly descended from a Scottish literary behemoth.

Major-General Sir Walter Maxwell-Scott was the great-great-grandson of Sir Walter Scott. In March 1937, he travelled to Franco-held territory in Spain on a fact-finding mission. Maxwell-Scott issued a statement upon his arrival home as he considered it 'only just to General Franco and to all Spaniards fighting with him to let the press and public know the following facts.' Those 'facts' amounted to a clear endorsement of Franco, and a denunciation of the republican government and its forces. Social policy had remained intact, according to Maxwell-Scott, as had the basic rate of wages. Food was plentiful, and republican prisoners relieved to have been captured and liberated. 'In other words', he wrote, 'General Franco is bound to win.' He continued:

The infiltration... of many thousands of volunteers has only helped to prolong the agony in Spain. A terrible responsibility lies on the shoulders of all those direct or indirect agents and sympathisers who, themselves safe at home, have sent over 50,000 'workers of the world' (not soldiers) to unite in death.

One year on, in March 1938, Maxwell-Scott called a meeting of establishment friends sympathetic to the Spanish nationalist cause. The result was the formation of a Scottish Friends of National Spain (FNS) branch under the tutelage of four vice-presidents, Maxwell-Scott himself, his wife Marie, Donald Cameron of Lochiel and Captain Luttman Johnson. The pro-Franco FNS, which had previously been restricted to activity in England only, set about making a mark in Scotland, successfully applying to Glasgow Corporation for permission to stage a meeting at St Andrew's Hall on 27 March.

On the 22nd, the Burgh Labour Party wrote a letter to the city's magistrates imploring them to reverse their decision to allow the FNS use of St Andrew's Hall. Protestations were also received from the Communist Party, local Co-operative societies and the Left Book Club. Citing fears over public order in the event of the meeting being staged, the magistrates acceded to their request. The FNS, however, vowed to hold the meeting regardless and expressed their incredulity at the magistrates' volte-face:

The sudden change of front has amazed the society, as no new circumstances have arisen. Some letters have been received by the magistrates apparently threatening violence. It seems that the magistrates' decision has proceeded from a fear of mob law and [an] inability to maintain order in their city.

A pamphlet outlining the BUF's vision of a corporate state modelled on the Italy of Benito Mussolini. Outside of Cathcart, the vision failed to gain significant support in Scotland.

Noting that magistrates' permission was not required for week night hire of the Hall, the FNS responded by craftily moving the date of their meeting to the following Thursday, 31 March. They had not reckoned upon the input of another council organ, the Halls Committee of the Corporation. The Halls Committee became the second body within two days to cancel the FNS meeting, reasoning that staging it would cause danger to St Andrew's Hall by provoking disorder and damage at the hands of rival groups. The General Finance Committee, however, overturned that decision by a single-vote majority, meaning the meeting could, in theory at least, now take place. The final decision rested with the councillors of the Glasgow Corporation.

Amidst this bureaucratic to-ing and fro-ing, political schisms had erupted within two of the three parties that made up Glasgow Corporation, as councillors advocating unbridled free speech clashed with those who wished to see pro-Franco groups subdued at any cost. The official position of the Socialist (an affiliated offshoot of the Labour Party) and Independent Labour parties was to deny the FNS any council premises for meetings. Yet within both parties' ranks sat a handful of avid proponents of free speech prepared to vigorously defend their position. The third component of the Corporation was made up by the Progressive Party, and their strict free speech ethos meant that dissenting ILP and Socialist voters could well determine votes on the matter.

On 31 March councillors met to decisively determine whether or not to approve Maxwell-Scott's request for meeting space. Their poll took place after a fierce debate in the City Chambers in which both sets of arguments were articulated. The motion to ban the FNS from using St Andrew's Hall was moved by Bailie Kerr, a Labour councillor representing Govan. He stated that even the 'shibboleth' of free speech should be bypassed on this occasion, and in blunt terms set out his argument to those present:

The point you are considering is whether or not you are going to give any opportunity to an association who are avowedly out to justify the brutalities of Franco in Spain, his butchering of the non-combatant population; a man whose hands are reeking with the blood of innocent women and children. Are we going to open our doors to any of them to allow them to justify the conditions that exist in Spain at the moment?

Indicating a split within the ranks, the main opponent of this statement was a fellow Labour councillor, Bailie Rosslyn-Mitchell, who highlighted the centrality of free speech in the history of British democracy:

It [free speech] is a spiritual essence. It is right down to the very blood and marrow of this nation that men who have thoughts should be free to express those thoughts; that whatever may be the opinion of those in authority, they shall not use their authority to prevent those who differ from them expressing that view.

It was to be Rosslyn-Mitchell's view that prevailed, with 51 councillors voting in favour of allowing the meeting, 38 against and 13 abstaining. The meeting had been given the green light on the very day it was to take place.

By that evening, anti-fascist protestors had gathered outside St Andrew's Hall creating a volatile atmosphere. Over 500 of the protesters ran through surrounding streets chanting 'down with Franco and the Labour traitors' until police employed force to disperse them. Many anti-fascists had obtained entrance tickets for the meeting and scuffles between them and the 150 FNS-employed stewards erupted at the start and continued throughout. About 1,500 people were in attendance to hear Maxwell-Scott and skier Arnold Lunn speak from the platform, though both were often drowned out by the din of protesters, some of whom unfurled a large red flag over the balcony. Lunn used his speech to deplore supporters of the Spanish republic, and refuted claims that civilians had been intentionally targeted in nationalist air raids:

There is a universe of difference between aiming badly at a factory for making aeroplanes and accidently hitting women and children and deliberately murdering women and children in cold blood.

Just as pro-republicans believed the Spanish Civil War was a rehearsal for a wider European war, Lunn believed it to be a rehearsal for the communist elimination of religion worldwide.

Two further FNS meetings were to follow. On 20 April, Maxwell-Scott told an audience at Glasgow's Central Hall of the fine and bounteous conditions in which Spaniards in nationalist territory now lived. When Franco was victorious, he said, there would be no fascism, merely a 'corporate' state like that of António de Oliveira

Sir Henry Lunn, supporter, along with his son Arnold, of the Friends of National Spain.

Salazar in Portugal. From June, the FNS attempted to establish a presence in Edinburgh, organising a meeting at Usher Hall for the 17th of that month. Despite explicit objections to the council from the local CPGB, the assembly went ahead in front of an audience of 500 people, 300 less than had turned out at the Mound on the previous night for a protest rally against the FNS.

The meeting was chaired by Perthshire-born Conservative MP Nairne Stewart-Sandeman, who claimed to have proof that the bombing of Guernica was undertaken entirely by land bombs, with no hint of an air attack. On a recent visit to Spain, he claimed to have seen no evidence of the persecution or massacre by Franco's forces of republicans in nationalist lands. Arnold Lunn's father Henry (founder of what became Lunn Poly travel agency), a Methodist minister, claimed that the FNS had the endorsement of all Scottish churches. In so doing, he neglected to mention Christian support for republican aid appeals. Women's police representative Mary Allen also addressed the floor, bursting with pride that she had been among the first foreign females to be invited by Franco to visit Spain during the civil war. To caterwauls from pro-republican spectators, a motion proposed by Allen congratulating 'General Franco and the Spanish people on their heroic and successful fight to maintain Christian civilisation, freedom, and religion in Spain' was then carried.

Following the meeting, the mood outside the Usher Hall on Lothian Road remained relatively calm. Breathing a collective sigh of relief, FNS members headed towards King's Stables Road, from where buses were to convey them home. But lying in wait there were several hundred anti-fascist protesters. Mayhem predictably ensued as the buses were halted in their progress by a determined crowd. Remarkably, only three arrests were made, all for the stoning of an FNS bus destined for Bannockburn.

Despite these open meetings, the FNS were never able to build popular support in Scotland and their movement slowly degenerated into a self-congratulatory gentleman's club for pro-Francoists. On 2 February 1939, the FNS held a banquet dinner at the Grosvenor Restaurant, Glasgow, to celebrate the fall to the nationalists of Barcelona. With Spanish flags draped on either side of a portrait of Franco, diners toasted impending nationalist victory, and guest of honour Charles Sarolea, a professor of French at Edinburgh University, claimed it would save 'us from a European catastrophe in the same sense as has Mr Chamberlain at Munich'. Evidently, prescience was not his strong point. Their party was interrupted, however, by four unwelcome guests. On hearing about the FNS dinner, former International Brigaders Robert Middleton and Hugh Eaglesham had booked a table for two at the Grosvenor. Whilst perusing the menus, they requested that their waiter introduce them to the FNS party. The men were informed that this would not be possible and upon protest were forced into a quiet room to receive a warning from the restaurant

The 1930s BUF's pamphlet *Break the Chains That Bind You*, an attack on Jewish financial influence, strongly echoing Nazi rhetoric.

manager. Meanwhile, two further ex-Brigaders, William McAulay and John McLean, had entered the Grosvenor and made the same request as Middleton and Eaglesham. The four men were then asked to leave, but instead began to chant 'down with Franco, arms for Spain', until eventually they were carried off by the police. In court, Eaglesham expressed his anger that the FNS should be celebrating what amounted to the slaughter of innocent women and children in Barcelona. All four were given the option of a £1 fine or 10 days in prison.

Whether on the streets or in upmarket restaurants, the FNS were unable to avoid working class protest. In this atmosphere, despite the clout of the Catholic church and some of its members, the aristocracy and sections of the press, Scotland's pro-nationalist movement was unable to flourish. Those motivated to oppose the Spanish republican side, whether through religious sympathy or admiration for Franco, were always in a minority, and by some distance. Scotland had already nailed its colours to the mast.

CHAPTER 11

The Red, Red Heart of the World: Scotland's 'Other' Left

Not filtered by the West
through the Guardian *digest*
but straight from the red, red heart of the world.
Willy Maley, 'On My Father's Refusal to Renew his Subscription to the *Beijing Review*'

THROUGH THEIR CENTRAL role in supporting the International Brigades and the aid movement, the Communists came to be the political party most associated with support for republican Spain. In Scotland, however, a number of other, smaller parties played their part in the campaign, some even sending personnel to serve in Spain.

An early defender of the Spanish republic was the Scottish Socialist Party (SSP). Formed by ILP members unhappy at their party's 1932 decision to disaffiliate from Labour, the SSP was part of the Britain-wide Socialist League. The SSP pledged itself to influencing Labour policy on Spain through continued affiliation, becoming something of a campaign group within the party. Though initially staunchly pacifist – leader Patrick Dollan told his party's 1934 conference that the SSP would 'under no circumstances take part in war' – the outbreak of war in Spain prompted a swift change of policy. The SSP harangued Labour over their early support for non-intervention, and became a leading voice in the campaign to grant the Spanish republicans the right to buy arms. They were, from the start of hostilities in Spain, a prickly thorn in Labour's side.

Similarly loyal to the Spanish republic was the Scottish Workers' Republican Party (SWRP), founded by John MacLean in 1923, the year of the great revolutionary's death. Ideologically, the SWRP sought to blend Marxism with nationalism, arguing that once nationalist revolution had occurred in one country, it could be exported elsewhere and a commonwealth of independent socialist nations created. Though this theory had been gestated with Scotland in mind, the party viewed it as applicable to Spain too. With the intention of protecting the republic and advancing a revolution, the SWRP wrote to left-wing groups in Spain to enquire as to how exactly they could assist:

At a workers' open forum here in Glasgow… The workers after assiduous discussion made it be known that they wish to come to Barcelona to help in the fighting on the Zaragoza front: they rank as ex-servicemen, as machine gunners, bomb throwers, rifleman, snipers and such. But what we want to know is how to get there, we have little idea: believe me, they are quite enthusiastic and bursting for further information. Please explain in detail.

Whether through lack of organisational knowledge or for other reasons, the SWRP were ultimately unable to send a group of their own to Spain, although some party members did travel on an individual basis or join the International Brigades. Though a small faction, the SWRP nonetheless contributed to the rich tapestry of the Scottish left and its seemingly intrinsic support of the Spanish republic.

Most influential of the 'other' parties was the ILP, which arguably contributed more to efforts for republican Spain than the Scottish Labour Party. Though officially a Britain-wide movement, the ILP was very much a Scottish party; its four members of the UK parliament elected in 1935 all represented Glasgow constituencies, and the party headquarters was situated in the city. Of those four MPs, two, James Maxton and John McGovern, became figureheads of its support for the republican side.

Maxton, described by political adversary Winston Churchill as 'the greatest parliamentarian of his day', wholeheartedly embraced the republican cause from the moment of Franco's attempted coup. It was said that if a doctor could have passed the 46-year-old fit, he would have been quick to join the fight. Maxton berated the British government's non-intervention policy, and accused the Chamberlain administration of allowing 'class prejudice' to prevent their aiding the republic. In 1937 he travelled to Spain to try to secure the release of ILP members taken prisoner there. For its duration, the war in Spain became Maxton's greatest fixation.

The ILP was essentially a revolutionary, Leninist party, although it rejected the dictatorial notion of democratic centralism. Unlike the Labour Party, the ILP condemned non-intervention from the start of the Spanish war, and rallied behind the Spanish republican side. Of the Scots who fought in Spain, as many as 100 were ILP members. A majority of them joined the International Brigades, although a number served in the ILP militia group made famous in the writings of George Orwell.

While the Communist Party and the leadership of the republican side agreed that revolution in Spain should be postponed and resources concentrated on defeating fascism first, the ILP believed that a revolutionary struggle should run parallel to the waging of war. This left them in ideological agreement with the POUM, and Spain's anarchists and their trade unions, for whom the Spanish Civil

War was a revolutionary war. The ILP and the POUM were also united by their anti-Stalinism, although neither group were Trotskyite, as they were commonly mislabelled.

When hostilities on the Spanish republican left over-spilled into internecine warfare in Barcelona in May 1937, the ILP sided firmly with the POUM and against the Communist-influenced troops of the republic. ILP figures in Barcelona identified the struggles of the POUM in Catalonia with their own in Scotland. John McNair, ILP representative in Spain, remarked that his young assistant Bob Smillie (see Chapter 12) 'thinks Barcelona is just like Glasgow!', and John McGovern MP wrote in the party's *New Leader* newspaper that 'Catalonia reminds me in many ways of my native Scotland'.

Six months previous to the fighting in Barcelona, the ILP had signed

John McNair, ILP representative in Spain

up to the CPGB-led Unity Campaign, though tensions in that relationship had begun to emerge in March 1937 at the party's annual conference. There, speakers raised doubts over the morality of maintaining relations with the Communists due to their role in Spain. One ILP member accused the Spanish Communist Party of plotting with the USSR and the CPGB to 'throttle the workers' revolution', while John McGovern castigated them for their 'lies' about the POUM, and labelled the *Daily Worker* the 'subsidised press of Stalin.'

Hostilities between the two parties were exacerbated when the ILP endorsed the POUM's rejection of the Spanish republic's Popular Front government. The POUM and ILP agreed that Spain should be run instead by a 'Workers' Front of Socialist Parties'. In a *New Leader* article published on 21 May, ILP figurehead Fenner Brockway wrote a lengthy editorial on the 'counter-revolution in Spain'. He contended that the Spanish Communist Party were now 'committed to the defence of property', and claimed that Soviet-facing Communist parties across the world had ceased to be revolutionary.

This dismissal of official doctrine led to the repression of the POUM in Spain and CPGB denouncements of the ILP in Britain. Following Barcelona's

East Fife MP Willie Gallacher, third from right, visits the ILP Contingent in Spain.

'civil war within a civil war', CPGB attacks on the ILP intensified, prompting the dissolution of the Unity Campaign in late May. The *Daily Worker* began to print vitriolic attacks on the ILP. An article published a day after Brockway's *New Leader* piece was tellingly entitled, 'Is the ILP winning the war or aiding Franco?' Referring to the POUM as the 'Spanish ILP', the article claimed that rank-and-file ILP members were opposed to their party's acquiescence with the Spanish group, and frothed:

> The Spanish ILP and the British ILP have eternally disgraced themselves by supporting a rebellion of anarchist uncontrollables at the very moment that Spanish rebellion is knocking at the gates of Bilbao.

A month later, in an article headlined 'Spanish Trotskyists Plot With Franco', the *Worker* alleged that the POUM leadership were in actual fact spies working within the republican movement for the nationalist leader. This attack on the POUM's actions in Spain was carried over to an attack on the ILP in Scotland in a CPGB circular. As figures who had 'supported, aided and defended' the POUM in their 'criminal acts' of 'sabotage' in Barcelona, the leadership of the ILP were endorsing the enemy of the republican struggle, according to the leaflet. 'For the ILP to come out in defence of the POUM', it raged, 'is a political crime against the Spanish people.' The CPGB emphasised the misdeeds of the POUM by invoking a hypothetical comparison with Barcelona events:

Suppose the Mosley Blackshirts were in control of the South-side of Glasgow and the North-side was governed by a Popular Municipal Council with the support of the great mass of the people, resolutely determined not only to prevent the Blackshirts from crossing the Clyde, but to advance and drive them out of the city. Suppose in such a situation the ILP, which had failed to play its part in the fight and retained their weapons in their homes and premises, started a revolt in Bridgeton and Shettleston calling for the overthrow of the Popular Council because they contended in represented capitalism, or for some other reason. Would it matter what the slogans of the revolt were? Its net effect would be to undermine the authority of the Council and aid the Blackshirts. Would it not be to the eternal disgrace of the Council if, in such a situation, it failed to crush the revolt and break up the organisation?

Written to justify the banning of the POUM on 16 June, in drawing a direct comparison between the Spanish party and the ILP, the CPGB were clearly escalating their campaign of condemnation against the Scottish party. While in Scotland Communist censure resulted in little more than a war of words, in Spain it had meant an often violent repression that David Murray referred to as a 'clamouring for the suppression, the liquidation, the annihilation of the POUM'. The battle raging on the left in Spain was also being played out in Scotland, albeit on a far lesser scale; the politics of Catalonia had been imported by Caledonia.

Direct ILP intervention in Spain came with the sending of a contingent of party members in early 1937. Prior to this, ILP representatives had already travelled to Spain and liaised with POUM colleagues, often clandestinely. A letter sent by John McNair in September 1936 to a Spain-bound ILP envoy identified only as Mr Martin captures the cloak and dagger atmosphere:

When you arrive at Perpignan go immediately to the Continental Bar, Place Araga, Perpignan. This is a restaurant and café where all the comrades meet and when you arrive there ask for Comrade J Canal. He will probably speak English. Give your letters to him and he will see that you get a Spanish workers' passport. In the small parcel attached is the famous packet of Players. There is a letter inside addressed to one of our comrades. The point is that this packet must be handed to a Spanish armed worker by you and not simply smoked in the office. You understand it isn't the value of the tabs, but the fact that one English workman gave them to us on that condition. If you could get a photo of this and send it on it would be excellent. Let them take photos on the spot of you and the ambulance. These photos will be reproduced in their paper *La Batalla* which we receive every day and we can then put them in our press here. Keep in the limelight as much as you can and get the stuff over to us. This publicity all helps us to raise money and carry on the good work.

Among the party of ILPers to join 'Mr Martin' in Spain at the start of the following year were several Scots, including Jock Ritchie, an ex-boxing champion from Lesmahagow, and Charles Doran, a Glaswegian veteran of World War One. They left London bound for Spain along with 23 other volunteers on 8 January. As they gathered at Victoria Station, the men sang the '*Internationale*' and a small crowd gathered to wish them farewell, although one woman shrieked: 'It is suicide for you all!'

Although 130 ILP members had volunteered to make the journey, the party leadership had decided to allow only unmarried men to travel. The initial contingent of 25 was viewed as a vanguard group later to be joined by 150 further volunteers (the day after they departed for Spain, the British government invoked the 1870 Foreign Enlistment Act and it appears the ILP made no further attempts to send fighting personnel.) In Barcelona, they were joined by Eric Blair (George Orwell), and Larkhall man Bob Smillie. The ILP contingent spent two weeks at the Lenin Barracks where they received training. In common with much of the instruction received by International Brigaders, rifle drill was completed in the absence of one major component: the rifle. In late January, the newly-created British section of the POUM militia departed for the Aragon Front via Lerida, where they met with John McNair. There, they were informed that they would be fighting as the 29th Lenin Division of the POUM Militia. In Aragon, they were stationed on hill slopes around 180 metres from nationalist front lines. Under the by-line 'Lesmahagow man in Spain', the *Lanark Gazette* reported with pride on the conditions faced by British section member Jock Ritchie:

The familiar accent of Lanarkshire was heard in the trenches of the Aragon Front when a Motherwell man, Mr David Murray, visited Jock Ritchie, ex-amateur heavyweight boxing champion of Scotland. 'Big Jock' was very calm and collected and as a bullet smashed into a sniper's post in a tree just overhead he remarked laconically 'they always shoot high anyway'. As they talked about the county, the besieged town of Huesca could be plainly seen about 500 yards away. Much nearer than that could be observed a line of loop-holed sandbags, in one of the enemy's positions. As a matter of fact at the point where Jock was anxiously awaiting his dinner, the rebel trenches were only a few yards away, well within a good biscuit or rather bomb toss.

However, the ILP contingent saw very little action indeed, sustaining only eight wounds between them in their entire time at the front. Most famously, Eric Blair was shot through the throat by a sniper during this time. A friend of Blair and his wife Eileen O'Shaughnessy, David Murray intimated in a 1955 letter that the author's wound was far from life-threatening, which suggested that artistic licence may have been at work in *Homage to Catalonia*. Murray wrote:

Shortly after he was wounded by a sniper near Siétamo on the Aragon Front, I saw Eric Blair walking about in Barcelona as large as life and quite the thing. In fact, I talked to him quite a bit.

As the suppression of the POUM entered its most brutal stage, the ILP contingent was hastily withdrawn from Spain. The men had been on leave in Barcelona when in-fighting broke out in early May, and some of them, including Blair, covered POUM headquarters from the roof of a theatre on the opposite side of the road. In late May, the ILP men were hurried out of Spain surreptitiously, thanks to the swift actions of party figures such as John McNair. For his part, McNair had been identified by the police as a wanted man, and spent his final two nights in Spain hiding alongside Eric Blair and Stafford Cottman, before the three, along with Blair's wife, were able to cross the border into France posing as rich tourists.

In his capacity as a freelance journalist specialising in articles on the steel industry, David Murray had visited Spain several times prior to the start of the conflict there. A fluent speaker of Spanish and German, his chief task during the civil war was to negotiate the release of POUM-sympathising prisoners, most famously Bob Smillie (see Chapter 12). He boasted to a Catalan friend and fellow linguist, Guillermo Neuman, that 'every child here [in Motherwell] knows what *No Pasaran* means now, and the phrase may pass into the English language.'

Murray also acted as a go-between for families and friends polarised by the conflict. He was a political campaigner of some brilliance, his biting prose style finding its way into the letters pages of many newspapers. Murray's indefatigable work attracted the admiration of John McNair, James Maxton (in spite of Murray's splenetic criticisms of his and John McGovern's praise of Neville Chamberlain following the Munich Peace deal) and many others on the non-communist left.

Before travelling to Spain for his work with prisoners, Murray had campaigned vigorously for the Spanish republic in his home country. In November 1936, he wrote to Neuman, describing a typical week:

Last week I gave three lectures on Spain, one to friends, one to a group of miners, one to a semi-religious group, all in the way of propaganda for the Spanish government. Then in addition to my ordinary work, I carry on newspaper correspondence with various Roman Catholic apologists.

He requested that Neuman should send him 'insignia of the militiamen' to put into a fundraising raffle, mentioning his recent success in raising funds from Motherwell railway workers, miners at Birkenshaw, Blantyre and Burnbank, and local Co-operative Men's Guilds. Murray's lecturing and fundraising tours took him to the Outer Hebrides. There, he drew out the parallels between the fight of the Spanish workers and peasants for land, liberty and education against the forces of landlordism and reaction, and the long drawn out struggle of the crofters and fishermen of the Long Island for the same things.

Unusually for an ILP man, Murray comfortably put aside his differences with the CPGB to work alongside them in campaigns for the International Brigades; for instance, in December 1937 he helped organise a concert at Motherwell Town Hall in which the Railway Clerks Association Mixed Voice Choir sang for 'the Dependents and Wounded Fund of the International Brigade'. He also became involved in the cross-party National Committee for Aid's food delivery service, devising a system whereby payments to Spanish consuls in Britain could be withdrawn as food parcels in Spain. More unconventionally, in February 1937, he launched a bid to provide a staple of the Scottish diet to soldiers and civilians in Spain. A press release detailed this innovative proposal:

The Independent Labour Party proposes to send a cargo of Scottish herring to Spain. Since most of the early Spanish potatoes are grown from Scottish seed, the loyal Spaniards will then be able to eat Scottish fish and chips.

The herring would be klondyked in bulk before being transported to a port in republican territory, where they would be exchanged for a cargo of oranges to be sold in Britain to meet expenses. This 'signal mark of solidarity' did not, surprisingly, breach the terms of the non-intervention agreement, and would be guaranteed a fairly safe passage:

A cargo of fish would be strictly permissible under the terms of the governmental non-intervention agreements and would be entitled to full protection from the Navy. At the same time a trawler is not so vulnerable to attack from submarines due to its small size and draft.

Sadly, the author has been unable to find any further trace of the 'Fish and Chips to Spain' plan, though this does not necessarily mean the idea never came into fruition.

In November 1938, Murray lent his support to another clever campaign, this time spearheaded by 22-year-old ILP members Adaline Campbell (whom he was later to marry) and Nancy Mac-Donald. They devised a scheme to flood the postal systems of Britain and France with food parcels for republican Spain, so compelling the two countries to break their own non-intervention policies. As Murray explained:

James Maxton MP, one of the ILP's most staunch supporters of the Spanish republican side.

If all party branches arranged to send parcels on a particular date the British and French non-interventionist governments would be forced to provide transport and to use their official machinery to supply food to Spain. The extra expense would be worth it for the propaganda effect.

As well as assisting in the export of goods to Spain, Murray was not immune to helping products make the opposite journey. As he informed Neuman: 'My friends and I require good quality caps. I have started the fashion of wearing the Basque bonnets in Motherwell.'

Murray's passage to Spain in May 1937 was smoothed after a Spanish potato importation board appointed him their Scottish representative (though this 'appointment' could well have been a cover story devised by the ILP and the POUM). In Spain, he worked for the release and wellbeing not only of POUM/ILP prisoners, but also for Scots accused of deserting from the International Brigades, including John Mudie, Malcolm Sneddon and James Donald (see Chapter 15).

As evidenced in his work with Mrs Lacey, George Keegan's mother, Murray acted as conduit for information between relatives in Scotland and men in their predicament. He also visited and supported Raisuli, the Moroccan brother-in-law of north African guerrilla leader Abd-el-Krim, who had been 'clapped in jail for no good reason.'

When Murray arrived back in Scotland, he was unhappy to find that, as he remarked in a letter to Neuman, 'All kinds of stories were circulating about me… I arrived to find myself famous, without cause. Being known is a nuisance to me.' This did not prevent him from continuing to wage political wars in newspapers and lecture halls. Unwanted notoriety was a price he was willing to pay for championing his principles.

The potency of these convictions was in evidence from the start of war in Spain. Murray was repeatedly disdainful about the inaction of the Labour Party ('timid and inactive') and the British government ('deplorable'). Having met with officials from the British Embassy and Consulate in Spain, Murray was left under no illusion that they were 'definitely pro-fascist and would rather help Franco supporters to get out of Spain than lend a hand with a real government supporter.' His antipathy was not reserved merely for the Labour Party and British establishment. As tensions between the communists and POUM in Spain grew, so too did his distaste for the CPGB and *Daily Worker*. On 8 July 1937, Murray wrote to the *Worker* in response to an article by Harry Pollitt, which he had read 'with utter disgust', seeing it as a 'gratuitous and venomous insult to the POUM and the ILP… from Pollitt's nasty remarks one would almost think that there are no POUM men in the trenches and that neither POUM nor ILP'ers have been wounded or killed.' He also suggested that Pollitt had glossed over disharmony in the ranks of the British Battalion:

He said nothing of the members of the British Battalion who are hiding in the Spanish ports waiting to get out of the country. He forgot the group of men who are left to rot in jail in Valencia, without even as much as a shirt on their backs. He omitted all mention of the wounded men who were abandoned in Barcelona to fend for themselves.

Murray went on to denounce Pollitt's article as merely a translation of a piece from the Spanish Communist Party's pro-Soviet *Frente Rojo* newspaper:

Until a few weeks ago, I had been a daily reader of your paper for years. Today I can hardly look at it; you have a positive genius for spleen, spite and studied insult. You will persist in getting in some wisecrack which has nothing to do with the point at issue.

Murray displayed similar scepticism about the Communist Party in an August 1937 letter to Mrs Lacey:

I saw Communist Party prisoners in jail with nothing else but their jacket and bags, for four or five months, not a shirt or pair of underpants. I have been very disappointed with the Communist Party both here and in Spain. They seem to have a craze for publicity and necessary jobs which bring no aura of glory are left undone. All the leaders want to be big shots and they have an enormous capacity for venomous insult.

In a later letter, he elucidated how his own political sympathies had been crystallised by what he saw in Spain:

I myself greatly admire the Spanish anarchists who are not the ruffians the papers here say, but are for the most part men of spirit and courage who have done most of the fighting. Today the Communist Party is going after them tooth and nail as the anarchists want a real revolution and the Communist Party are only out for parliamentary democracy which is just what we have here. Imagine all that precious blood being spilt for nothing.

However caught up Murray was in the squabbles that dogged the republican side, unlike many others, he was able to put his own opinions aside and, as he wrote to Guillermo Neuman in November 1937,

remain firmly on the side of the legal government as the confusion which accompanies every social upheaval is nothing compared with the organised murder of Franco and his hoards of foreigners. There may have been injustices on the government side but on the other side there is mass terrorism and murder.

Murray placed the importance of republican unity over personal reservations and his sense of the 'greater good' is reflected in the countless missives he fired off in remonstration with anti-republican newspapers. Typical was a fiery letter written in August 1938, reacting to a *Glasgow Herald* article that had played down Franco's fascist credentials:

It is amazing how so many people like your correspondent continue to believe that the mission of the rebel General Franco is to preserve his country from communism. Last year I met in Valencia a very highly-placed British official who believed much the same thing and did not bother to hide his pro-Franco sympathies. I met the same person a few weeks ago after he had returned from a year in rebel territory. His views had completely changed. He informed me that the people under Franco's domination were sullen, that oppression was rife and that executions took place continually. He confirmed that all the essential services in rebel Spain are under the control of Germans and Italians. The railways, the posts and the telegraphs are run by Germans and the whole country is rapidly becoming a Nazi colony.

Murray, who found common ground with the wider republican left in deploring the role of the Catholic church in Spain, made this parting shot:

It is a pity Franco has so many supporters in this country, and still more a great pity that they masquerade mostly as Christian patriots with a civilising mission and often get away with it.

He believed that a victory for Franco would mean a restoration of the Catholic church's power, and therefore that, as he later wrote, 'Spain would be pushed back to the time of Columbus.' 'Spain under clerical-fascist domination', Murray argued, 'will be a mass cemetery.'

For all his public campaigning, Murray did not relish attention for its own sake, but his role in investigating the 'murder' of Scottish ILP volunteer Bob Smillie was to push him fully into the limelight.

PART 3
Spanish Stories, and Endings

CHAPTER 12

Murder or Circumstance?
The Bob Smillie Story

*His lilting Scottish melodies could often be heard enlivening many
difficult and monotonous hours. I can hear his voice now as he shouted
slogans in Spanish from our trenches in the Aragon mountains across
to the enemy lines. Was it merely coincidence that at this period 100
Spanish workers deserted from Franco?*

Bob Edwards, ILP contingent member and later Co-operative and Labour MP

BORN IN 1917, Robert Ramsay Smillie was the grandson of Robert Smillie,
a Larkhall miners' leader who later became a Labour MP. Known as 'Bob',
the young Smillie had grown up in a militant ILP land-working family, their
left-wing politics as assured as their grinding poverty. James Maxton wrote of
Smillie and his background:

We knew the stock from which he came. We saw his father and mother
living a strenuous existence on their little farm in Lanarkshire, toiling
early and late on the soil, but still with surplus energy to devote to the
socialist movement, to the unemployed, to the improvement of the
conditions of the miners living around them.

Smillie joined hunger marches as an 18-year-old. He opposed rearmament
and war and opined that the establishment of world socialism was the only
method of achieving peace. He worked to create an ILP version of the Young
Communists' League, resulting in the formation of the Guild of Youth.

When the war in Spain began, Smillie threw himself into the fray. In October
1936, he broke off from a chemistry degree at Glasgow University to travel
to Barcelona, where he joined the Executive Committee of the International
Revolutionary Youth Bureau, and became John McNair's assistant.

Smillie transferred the energies he had ploughed into his work for the ILP
across to the POUM. As James Maxton stated, he endorsed their perspective
on the conflict in Spain, viewing

the Spanish struggle *not* as one between capitalist-democracy and
fascism, but rather as the struggle of the Spanish working class against

the forces of fascism *and* international capitalism; with the hope of ultimate victory for the Spanish people, with the hope of the foundation of a Soviet Spain.

In a letter home to fellow ILP member Dan McArthur, Smillie declared his loyalty to the POUM youth section on the grounds that they stood for 'the social revolution and *not* for the democratic republic'. This placed him in direct opposition to the stated position of the Popular Front government, the Communist Party and his compatriots in the International Brigades.

Smillie dedicated himself to his propagandistic and support roles in Barcelona, but when the ILP contingent of volunteers arrived in Spain in January 1937, he demanded to be sent to fight alongside them. Permission was reluctantly granted (McNair and others had reservations about letting such a young man enter the field of battle), and Smillie joined his colleagues in their journey to the Aragon Front. In action, he fought bravely, gaining the praise of POUM and ILP leaders, including Commander Georges Kopp, who wrote:

> We have had a complete success, which is largely due to the courage and discipline of the English [sic] comrades who were in charge of assaulting the principal of the enemy's parapets. Among them I feel it my duty to give a particular mention to the splendid actions of Eric Blair [George Orwell], Bob Smillie and Paddy Donovan.

At the end of April, Smillie and the ILP contingent travelled to Barcelona for a period of leave. The young volunteer was issued a permission document from a POUM official permitting his return to Scotland 'for very grave family reasons, which in my judgement and because of his excellent record warrant his temporary absence.' In the second week of May, Smillie began his journey home, heading north towards the Pyrenees. He was to attend a meeting of the International Bureau in Paris on the 11th, before continuing his campaign work for the Guild of Youth with a speaking tour of Scotland. This plan suggests that the 'grave family reasons' may have been fabricated to ensure his smooth exit from Spain. Yet on 10 May, he found himself under arrest at Figueras. David Murray explained the initial reasoning given for Smillie's detention:

> He had no written permit in his possession to leave the militia and to pass over the frontier. He had such a permit signed by the commander of the Lenin Division but had unfortunately forgotten it in Barcelona.

Smillie later reported a feeling that the authorities had been 'waiting for him' in Figueras. After a custodial night in the increasingly volatile atmosphere of Barcelona, he was swiftly transferred to the Model Prison in Valencia. It was clear that Smillie had become a victim of the government's POUM clampdown, as David Murray testified:

> Unfortunately, young Smillie was arrested at the exact time of the crisis in the Valencia government, and no definite steps could be taken to have him released during the period of flux.

A police statement confirmed that Smillie had been detained on three counts: for lacking the certificate allowing him out of Spain; for carrying 'documents'; and for having 'materials of war' about his person. All three charges were specious: Smillie did have the required pass but had left it behind as David Murray stated; the documents he carried were merely personal letters (including messages of love to his girlfriend Catriona that the republican authorities saw fit to translate); and he was in possession of two hand grenades, both of which were discharged and intended as war souvenirs.

David Murray was immediately assigned to the case of his 'brither Scot' by the ILP. By the time Murray visited Smillie in his barren cell at the Model Prison, the young Scot had talked his way into a further, more serious charge of 'rebellion against the authorities'. This charge arose when, in questioning, Smillie had naively admitted to being in the POUM building during Barcelona street fighting on 3 May. That he had played no active part in the skirmishing did not matter; association was enough to merit an indefinite prison term. Police suspicions of Smillie had been heightened by sensationalist press coverage in Britain and Spain, and the communist-influenced authorities began to think that they had captured a figure of great importance to the POUM and ILP (despite the fact Smillie played a vital role in the youth wings of both parties, at 20 years old he had not yet reached anything like the highest echelons of power). Though Smillie was arrested prior to the main wave of repression against the POUM and their associates, he could not escape the repercussions of the embittered political climate outside the prison walls; the increased charges against him reflected that much.

ILP efforts to secure Smillie's release had begun the moment news of his arrest emerged. On 11 May, John McNair appealed to the British consulate for help and continued to lobby them over the following weeks. David Murray also looked to the consulate for assistance, but ended up frustrated and convinced, as we have seen, that the British authorities were inherently pro-nationalist. The POUM also swung into action, lobbying the Spanish authorities and producing a replica of Smillie's original exit certificate, though all they received in reply from the police service was a perfunctory note stating that nothing could be done. Murray and the POUM engaged a solicitor, Vincente

Martinez Ubreros, to work on the case. Ubreros and Murray were successful in gaining access to Smillie, and visited him several times in prison, where Murray also met with deserters Donald, Mudie and Sneddon.

Murray wrote to the ILP leadership in late May to convey his exasperation at coverage of the Smillie case in the *New Leader*, and to reason that the arrest of the man had arisen due to misunderstandings:

> In spite of the foolish *New Leader* comments, Smillie carried no documents and was arrested purely by chance. He and his Barcelona and London friends have been his own worst enemies and I promise them all a good kick in the pants. The military police recognises that the whole thing is a piece of nonsense but the 'secret' police are said to be engaged in investigating the circumstances.

At this stage, it appeared that an end to the case would swiftly follow; yet as June began, Smillie was still in detention without charge. Not wishing to prejudice the case or give the nationalists an opportunity to spread negative publicity, the ILP chose to remain outwardly quiet on the matter. However, behind the scenes, James Maxton and the party head office pleaded for help from the Spanish Ambassador in London and asked other figures in the labour movement to do the same.

On Friday 4 June, Smillie complained of stomach pains that were to worsen over the weekend. On Sunday 6th, he finally received medical attention, albeit from a fellow inmate who was a qualified doctor. But as the week progressed, Smillie's condition deteriorated rapidly, until his cell-mate, a Spaniard named Vincente Rodriguez, insisted that the Scot be taken to the prison hospital. Smillie was diagnosed with appendicitis. Ward congestion meant he could not be operated upon. Hearing of his friend's decline in health, David Murray travelled to Valencia from his office in Barcelona on 11 June. By the time he arrived in the city, Smillie had been transferred to Valencia's provincial hospital. Arriving out of hours and with no medical records, he was left unattended for some time and subsequently fell into a coma. Murray was informed that Smillie was conscious and had indicated that he did not wish to receive any visitors. When on the evening of Saturday 12th June a doctor finally examined him, it was found that, owing to congestion in his lower abdomen, he could not be operated upon. What happened next was described in a note written by Murray after the event:

> Smillie came in [to the theatre] about 11pm. Doctor against operation as already too late. Bob got up out of bed, staggered and fell, hitting his head. Was dead two hours after arrival. Advanced peritonitis.

However, as Smillie breathed his last, Murray remained unaware of the young Scotsman's plight. On Sunday 13th, he wrote to Minister of Justice Manuel Irujo asking him to intervene in Smillie's case 'either to procure immediate release of the prisoner or to expedite the legal investigation and trial'. He also penned a fairly upbeat letter to Smillie himself, again emphasising that the clearing of misunderstandings brought on by the detainee would prompt an annulment of charges:

Robert Smillie MP, grandfather of Bob Smillie.

You seem to have been bent on giving all the wrong answers to the questions put to you. You would have been out long ago but for your own actions and those of your well meaning friends. You have been accused out of your own mouth – due, of course, to your faulty knowledge of Spanish, and to your misunderstanding of the question put to you. The whole business is an unfortunate mistake.

On 14 June, convinced he was just a few more meetings away from obtaining Smillie's release, Murray travelled to the Model Prison only to be greeted with the news of his death. That morning at 10am, Robert Ramsay Smillie, not yet 21 years old, had been buried in a wooden casket at Valencia's giant main cemetery. It was left to Georges Kopp to pay tribute to Smillie in a letter to his parents:

You have by this time heard of the sad and untimely fate of your son, Robert. He was one of the most gallant soldiers in the regiment which I commanded. It is a duty and a privilege to express to you my sympathy, and to assure you that Bob always carried himself bravely and courageously in and out of the firing line. You can be proud of him.

From the moment news of Smillie's fate became public, conspiracy theories about the circumstances of his arrest and death began to mount. From the beginning, David Murray insisted that Smillie had been arrested on a technicality and then died of natural causes, although he did admit that the republican authorities were slow in treating him, with fatal consequences. Murray was repeatedly forced to deny the accusation that Smillie had been arrested and murdered because he held secrets the republicans did not want revealing, and for his collusion with the POUM. On 30 June he wrote to John McNair:

The opinions which are widely current that Robert Smillie was arrested due to a suspected connection with secret conspiracies and planned outrages is quite unfounded. Accusations that the prisoner was ill treated and finally shot are completely untrue.

In a message to Eileen O'Shaughnessy the next day, Murray reported:

All kinds of rumours are circulating; that he had bombs, papers from Franco and even that he was going to blow up churches. Others state that he was shot and buried secretly. The facts are that he was arrested for having no discharge papers on him. He had neither documents nor bombs and there never was any prospect of a charge along these lines.

Alex Smillie, Bob's father, initially accepted Murray's account of events. On 28 July, he wrote, 'I am well satisfied that my son died from one of these causes which human beings cannot avoid', and Murray wrote to John McNair, 'The Smillies are bearing up very well... you must remember they are not fushionless Sassenachs and thus not easily beaten.'

Yet by the winter of 1937, Alex Smillie had begun to doubt Murray's version of events. He now believed the accusations made in newspaper articles by Ethel MacDonald that his son had been targeted by the secret police and executed. Characteristically open and frank, in responding to Smillie senior's misgivings Murray pledged to answer 'anything within the orbit of my personal knowledge or experience.' He continued:

I am convinced, and this I can affirm on oath, that Bob died a natural death. All my observations and impressions lead me to this conclusion. Judgement is a human thing and liable to error, but in spite of every curious and mysterious circumstance, I am convinced that Bob was never ill-treated nor was he done to death.

Coming from a man as honourable as Murray, this statement was not to be taken lightly. 'I am sorry to have to bring these matters up,' he continued, 'but complete openness is the only thing to counter the wild and unfounded statements which are gaining currency.' Despite this avowed candidness, Alex Smillie now accused Murray of suppressing relevant facts. At an ILP conference in February 1938, he aired his grievances in public, heckling Murray as he spoke from the podium. Testing his patience further, a delegate also approached Murray and accused him of being a spy for the *Daily Express*. Murray wrote to John McNair:

> I had no intention of mentioning the Smillie case except to say that a report was on the way. Alex Smillie immediately jumped up and shouted that if I were to be allowed to speak he would demand the right also then he went on to shout about 'suppression'. I had to go to another meeting and I told our local lad to tell Alex that I had not intended to refer to Bob's case. He said to the Motherwell chap 'you don't know the lies David Murray has been telling me'.

Murray contacted Smillie the day after the conference, again emphasising that nothing had been kept from him. In reply, Smillie claimed that the true facts of the case were hidden in Murray's file, destined never to appear in any reports. This supposition was based on perceived inconsistencies between Murray's early comments on Smillie's death and official reports later released by the ILP stating that it had been a tragic accident:

> I am not pursuing this case gladly, but I have a duty to the boy who, according to your first statement in Barcelona, was 'murdered' by the people in charge at Valencia... you completely fail to draw the conclusions from the evidence which everyone else draws who has seen it.

Smillie wrote that he had initially delayed coming forward with his suspicions because of his high regard for Murray and loyalty to the ILP. Highly regarded or not, Murray still faced the task of once again refuting Smillie's accusations, and he duly obliged, in impassioned terms:

> I insist that I have consciously tried to get to the bottom of the whole matter, that I have suppressed nothing, that I have added nothing and that I thoroughly believe what I have stated. I do not for a moment deny that individuals were guilty of gross neglect and carelessness and I do not believe there was any conspiracy to get Bob, to ill treat him, and then to do away with him.

Of particular vexation to Murray was the charge by Alex Smillie and others that Bob had been a political prisoner, thus hypothetically paving the way for his ill-treatment at the hands of the republican secret police. Having visited the Model Prison, though, Murray was able to affirm to Alex that

WE CARRY ON

Our tribute to

BOB SMILLIE

By DAN McARTHUR

With a Foreword by
JAMES MAXTON, M.P.

ONE PENNY
I.L.P. GUILD OF YOUTH, 35 ST. BRIDE STREET, LONDON, E.C.4

A pamphlet in remembrance of Bob Smillie.

his imprisonment was no secret and all the particulars were entered quite openly into the books of the Military Fiscal. I saw them and he was purely a military prisoner.

While Murray believed that Smillie's incarceration was prolonged as a consequence of political events, he was adamant that the initial arrest had been purely down to military factors, namely the homeward bound Scot misplacing his discharge certificate. Smillie had fallen victim to the republican authorities' clampdown on desertion from active service in Spain. Alex Smillie continued to doubt his version of events, though ultimately he decided not to take the case further. He later contributed to the ILP's official report on the case.

Alex Smillie's suspicions were undoubtedly stoked by the conspiracy theories that gained credence in left-wing circles, many of which still make for intriguing reading today. Belgian POUM commander Georges Kopp, himself arrested on 19 June 1937, did not make an official statement on the matter until January 1939. Kopp was adamant that Bob Smillie had been kicked to death by the SIM. During his own cross-examination by the SIM, Kopp claimed to have noticed a filing cabinet containing dossiers on figures suspected of working for or with the POUM. On being left alone in the room, he had investigated further and seen that among them there was a file on Bob Smillie. Upon Kopp's release in late September 1937, he decided to burgle the fairly unsecure unit in which he had been questioned, and take possession of the Smillie file. Having done so, he pored through the details of the file before sending it to his mother in Belgium for safe-keeping, though it was never to arrive there. According to Kopp, it contained around 200 pages of statements detailing a cross-examination of Smillie undertaken by SIM agents on 12 June. In his January 1939 statement, he attested that, during this examination Smillie had been informed

that a fascist plot had been discovered in England and that the ILP was compromised in it; that the English police had found out that Fenner Brockway and John McNair were mere fascist agents, actually on the pay-roll of the Gestapo; that the POUM was a fascist organisation too and was about to be crushed.

Smillie was then asked to sign a statement condemning the POUM and the ILP. He replied that he was happy to sign any statement against fascism upon the production of evidence of the POUM/ILP plots. Smillie had refused to sign a number of statements placed in front of him by the SIM agents, until the police told him that he would have to be 'taught to behave better'. The final statement in the file, by a doctor, stated that the 'teaching' had rapidly got out of hand, necessitating Smillie's urgent transfer to hospital. Kopp recounted:

The doctor states that Bob had the skin and the flesh of his skin perforated by a powerful kick delivered by a foot shod in a nailed boot; the intestines were partly hanging outside. Another blow had severed the left side connection between the jaw and the skull and the former was merely hanging on the right side. Bob died about 30 minutes after reaching the hospital.

In the context of David Murray's official verdict that Smillie had died from peritonitis, these were startling allegations which directly contradicted it. The story also fitted in with Murray's initial report of Smillie having 'a bang on his head', albeit not from a fall. But could all those inmates of the Model Prison who told Murray they had witnessed Smillie's illness and deterioration have been lying? And how could Kopp's memory be so precise after a brief glance at 200 pages of reports in Spanish? Also, where had the Smillie dossier disappeared to?

Well before Kopp's statement was issued, Ethel MacDonald had fanned the flames of conjecture with her own hypothesis. On her return from Spain in November 1937 after a spell as representative of the United Socialist Movement (USM), she did her utmost to convince the public that Bob Smillie had been murdered, alleging that the secret police had assassinated him in cold blood. Many in Spain at the time also believed this, to the extent that even ILP insider Charlie Doran was convinced Smillie had been shot. MacDonald also claimed that Smillie had been secretly buried under a different, possibly Belgian, name. Her accusations infuriated the ILP leadership. John McNair summed up the mood when he wrote to party member Hugh McNeill, 'Ethel MacDonald knows nothing about the case of our Comrade Bob and my feeling is that this cheap publicity is both uncalled for and painful.'

A letter to McNair of January 1938 shows how David Murray worked to counter her statements and question their veracity:

> Ethel MacDonald has been quite a trouble and my tactics are to choke
> her off. I corrected her second article for the *Sunday Mail*. It was full of
> errors – Bob's age, my visit to Spain, in fact everything. I might have let
> it go and then slammed her but once a thing appears in print any amount
> of contradiction will not remove the impression.

MacDonald also insisted that Smillie had been carrying out anti-communist
activities on behalf of the POUM. Murray worried that 'this is just what the
Communist Party is looking for as a cause for action'; in MacDonald's words,
they would find justification for reprisals against the POUM. Her contentions,
though, were never really taken as statements of fact; the greatest damage they
caused was in adding to the rumour-mongering surrounding Smillie's death.

Perhaps MacDonald's claims of wrongdoing would have gained more
credence than they did had she eschewed the political angle and focused on
medical issues alone. Here, there were a number of apparent inconsistencies.
In a letter to Alex Smillie, Dr A Ferrer, the consultant with responsibility
for Bob following his arrival in Valencia Hospital, confirmed that the patient
had died from acute peritonitis. Dr Ferrer had taken the decision that 'it
was pointless to operate, and it only would have made his condition worse.'
Smillie's plight was already, in his view, irreversible. His death had been one
of those 'very unfortunate events that we all wish would never happen.' Ferrer
claimed that when Smillie had left the prison hospital he was 'very satisfied
with his treatment, to the extent that when he was discharged... he shook the
[prison] doctor's hand and had a smile on his face.'

This directly contradicts the statements of other witnesses, who claimed
Smillie left the prison hospital in a dire condition, rendering an exchange of
pleasantries unlikely. David Murray was told by Model Prison inmate John
Mudie that prior to his transfer to the provincial hospital, Smillie's face had
been a 'terrible red', and his entire body 'practically useless.' He was clearly in
an advanced state of neglect, largely because, said Mudie, the 'prison official
doctor apparently did not want to do anything' (the POUM even claimed that
the communist secret police had effected this delay and hence caused Smillie's
death). Further, the stricken Smillie had left the prison hospital under his own
steam, as Murray wrote in his initial report, 'The prison authorities were
guilty of grave neglect. Bob was not *taken* or *carried* to the hospital but was
compelled to stagger there himself.'

It seems clear that Smillie was in no fit state to bid a fond farewell to the
prison hospital and its staff. While this does not disprove the fact he died
of peritonitis, it does show that certain aspects of the official statement on

Smillie's death were questionable. It is easy to see why Alex Smillie and others felt that all was not as it seemed.

Suspicions over the death of Bob Smillie were expressed in George Orwell's *Homage to Catalonia*, first published in April 1938, in which he referred to Smillie as 'perhaps the best of the bunch' among the ILP contingent.[25] Orwell felt he had died 'an evil and meaningless death... like a neglected animal' and was sceptical in the extreme as to what caused it, writing 'perhaps the appendicitis story was true... [but] people so tough as that do not usually die of appendicitis if they are properly looked after.' Orwell's take on proceedings was written before the release of the ILP's official report into Smillie's death, which, to an extent justified his comments. Rather than offering an alternative explanation for the death, Orwell's words stood to reinforce the ILP's official line: Smillie had been the victim of a tragic case of neglect.

That official line was reached following extensive investigatory work by David Murray, who took statements from inmates, medical staff and wardens in the Model Prison, as well as from patients, nurses and doctors at the provincial hospital. He also interviewed the Military Fiscal and staff at the Office of Public Safety, the Ministry of Justice and the SIM. With his journalistic background shining through, Murray even carried out interviews at the mortuary and the cemetery where Smillie was interned. His report was completed in February 1938, and published in the *New Leader* newspaper on 11 March.

Reflecting the position that David Murray had taken from the outset, it held that Smillie had been arrested not for political reasons but for failing to carry a discharge certificate with him when attempting to leave Spain. However republican authorities had sought to establish whether Smillie had played a part in POUM agitation, prolonging his stay in prison and belatedly adding a political element to his incarceration. The report made it clear that Smillie was perfectly innocent of any wrongdoing and suggested that had he lived, he would have been released. The report concluded:

> We consider that Bob Smillie's death was due to great carelessness on the part of the responsible authorities which amounted to criminal negligence.

Interestingly, an earlier version of Murray's findings, included in a July 1937 letter to John McNair, included 'intent' as a possible motive for the neglect shown to Smillie when his illness had become serious. After hearing evidence, Murray was confident that there had been no deliberate delay in treating Smillie. 'There was', he wrote, 'no secret about the manner of his arrest, his place of imprisonment, the type of illness, the location of the hospital and the place of the burial.'

Questions still hang over the probity of this conclusion. It has been suggested that Murray removed the 'intent' part of the argument so as to avoid reigniting tensions on the republican left while the civil war was still being fought. He had been the man closest to the case, and in later years he consistently maintained that there was no sense in the argument that the Spanish would want to kill the young grandson of a titan of the trade union movement. In 1955, Murray, now a Liberal, responded to a letter in the *Evening Times* that once again cast doubt over Smillie's fate, replying for what must have seemed like the millionth time:

> Young Robert Ramsay Smillie was not 'captured and thrown into prison'. On the way home for a speaking tour he was detained at Figueras because his papers were not in order. It happened to be a troublous time so that the detention was not out of the way. He took peritonitis in the Model Prison in Valencia, died in the General Hospital in that city and was buried in the local cemetery. It was all very sad but it could have happened to anyone.

His adult life barely begun, Smillie had been laid to rest in a land he had sought to defend from fascism and bring revolution to. A Valencian doctor wrote to his father in moving recognition of his sacrifice:

> Your son is buried in the beautiful land of Valencia, a land of brilliant sun and of wide and glorious scenes. His body rests in a land where love of liberty and of democracy are part and parcel with communal life. Now that he is dead, he has the gratitude of the Spanish people, who will never forget those who left their good and peaceful life in their own country to separate themselves from their families and to join the defenders of liberty and independence in Spain.

CHAPTER 13

The Scots Scarlet Pimpernel: Ethel MacDonald

If this journey does not make me do something worthwhile, nothing will. I feel that my future centres round here. I am optimistic. I am alive and I am prepared to risk everything in order to be alive. I am here and I shall not return from this land of struggle and heroism in our cause without making an effort to serve.

Ethel MacDonald, Radio Barcelona speech, March 1937

ETHEL MACDONALD'S STANCE on the case of Bob Smillie arose from her own experiences in Spain. MacDonald was invited to the country in October 1936 by the CNT-FAI trade union federation, owing to her work with the anarchist United Socialist Movement, another Scottish party with political interests in the civil war.

The USM was formed in 1934 by Guy Aldred, a leading British anarchist, along with MacDonald, John Taylor Caldwell and anti-parliamentarian members of the ILP. Based in the Bakunin Hall on Glasgow's Stirling Road, the USM was an anarcho-socialist party. Their ideology borrowed heavily from the theories of William Morris, with a belief in workers' councils and direct action over democratic political parties. Over the course of the civil war, they held meetings on the subject in Glasgow and Edinburgh and hosted exhibitions of Spanish anarchist art. Aldred had planned to send a 'USM Anti-Parliamentary Delegation and Expedition' to Spain in September 1936, to join up with anarchist militia groups and enter the military fray. However, the USM found gathering funds for the 'expedition' difficult. They mounted a plea for money in their own *Regeneracion* newspaper on 3 October:

> Many readers could help us. Some could advance all the money needed. The delegation must leave within one week. Will comrades make a special effort, by loans and donations? If this delegation and expedition is delayed unduly, the Anti-Parliamentarians will prove themselves to be as futile and as contemptible as the Parliamentarians.

Donations proved insufficient and in February 1937 Ethel MacDonald was still awaiting the arrival of her comrades, as she remarked in a letter to Aldred:

Do you remember the proposal about sending a battalion of 50 anarchists from Glasgow? I think you had better start getting your list ready. But they must be *anarchists* or *anti-parliamentarians*! This is essential.

Bereft of the financial clout enjoyed by large membership parties such as the CPGB, the USM's efforts ultimately came to nothing. MacDonald and her friend Jenny Patrick were destined to be the only USM representatives in Spain.

Ethel Camilia MacDonald was born in Bellshill in 1909. A working class woman of some erudition, she became local ILP secretary in her teens, and became fluent in French and German. Aged 16, she had been sent by the labour exchange for a waitressing job in Dumfries. On arrival, finding that it did not exist, she solicited the advice of Guy Aldred, a locally renowned activist. Impressed by MacDonald's revolutionary zeal and political acumen, Aldred appointed her secretary for his Anti-Parliamentary Communist Federation. She took on the same position in the USM upon its inception and was to serve Aldred and the cause until her death from multiple sclerosis in 1960.

MacDonald and Jenny Patrick, Aldred's wife, were summoned to Barcelona to work in the CNT-FAI's foreign language information centre, and later give nightly English-language political broadcasts on Radio Barcelona. They travelled to Spain in early November 1936. In her diary, Patrick recorded the joy felt by the two upon their arrival in Barcelona:

Tuesday, 3rd November was the most exciting day in both of our lives and I don't think we'll ever forget it. We handed in our papers and after they realised we were comrades, they were terribly nice to us. They asked us if we had money and we told them the truth that we were broke. They took us to a restaurant and we had a wonderful time. Everyone was bright and cheerful and happy. So naturally we were the same. We felt full of enthusiasm. This was revolution.

Writing in the *Sunday Mail* on 5 December, MacDonald could not contain her own early zest for the vigour of Catalan life:

In the main square, the Plaza de la Republica, the white walls of the Generalitat, the government offices, glistened in brilliant sunshine. Birds were singing in the trees and the sky was the most beautiful blue that I have ever seen. Civilian soldiers dressed in their inevitable dungarees and little red and black Glengarry bonnets and smoking endless cigarettes, strolled casually in Las Ramblas and the Via Durruti or chatted to the girl soldiers in the Plaza Catalunya. We had difficulty deciding which were young men and which were girls. They were dressed exactly alike, but as we drew nearer we saw that all the girls had beautifully permed hair and were strikingly made up.

Despite this fervour, the women initially struggled to find a practical role in fomenting revolution as they had wished. They were also troubled by financial difficulties, a CNT loan having failed to materialise. In a joint letter to Guy Aldred, the pair outlined their anxieties:

Perhaps things may brighten tomorrow and be OK. You know how bad things seem sometimes on first impressions and then come alright. Anyhow we intend to stick it out, if we can get anything at all to do, whether useful or not, as we don't want to return like bad pennies. It would be more pleasant if we felt we had some sort of niche, could really be of some use.

MacDonald wrote in her diary (later serialised in the *Bellshill Speaker*) on 20 November of her plans to become 'a speaker, an able and intelligent speaker and not just one who speaks'. Yet it was through the written word that MacDonald, along with Patrick, first found 'some sort of niche' and, indeed, prominence. Their crowning glory as journalists occurred during May 1937, when they became probably the first foreign writers to report the internecine street fighting rocking Barcelona. In the *Barcelona Bulletin*, circulated around Glasgow, MacDonald and Patrick's eyewitness account startled the left in Scotland and beyond. Dated 5 May, their report was graphic:

The trouble broke out on Monday afternoon. The civil guards seized the telephone building by force. As the move was quite unexpected, they succeeded in disarming the militiamen in charge there, and so gaining control. All during the night there was firing in the street, and we had a good view from the hotel windows. As the day [Tuesday] wore on the firing became terrific: the police were firing from their building further up the street, and from nearby houses, and the CNT were replying from their HQ, from the balconies and from the roof. The noise is terrible, and already there have been many killed and wounded.

For her own part, MacDonald had embarked upon her quest to become 'an able and intelligent speaker' in January, beginning work as a presenter on the CNT-FAI-run Barcelona Radio. Her nightly broadcasts achieved the substantial feat of becoming an anarchist version of Franklin D Roosevelt's comfy 'fireside chats' in America. Indeed, so pleasing were MacDonald's tones, she courted

SAVE SPAIN. ACT!

RADIO SPEECHES BY ETHEL MacDONALD

GLASGOW, 1st MAY, 1937.   ONE PENNY.

A newspaper collection of Ethel MacDonald's Radio Barcelona speeches, published in Glasgow on May Day 1937.

unlikely support from that country in the form of regular fan mail, as the *Glasgow Herald* reported:

A prominent news editor in Hollywood says that he has received hundred of letters concerning Ethel MacDonald, stating that the writers, in all parts of the USA and Canada, enjoyed her announcements and talks from Barcelona radio, not because they agreed with what she said, but because they thought she had the finest radio speaking voice they had ever heard.

MacDonald covered a wide range of topics relating to left-wing politics in her transmissions and displayed an ability to disseminate complex ideas in coherent and lively language, as demonstrated in this segment from a speech chiding the British government's ban on volunteers to Spain and attempting to incite retaliatory action:

Are you, English-speaking workers, prepared to let this tragic force which means the rape of Spain go on? Are you prepared to lend yourself to this mockery? Are you willing to be fooled longer in this fashion? If you are men and women, if you sense class struggle, you will permit no ban on volunteers.

MacDonald's orations were often critical of the communist-influenced republican government and the parliamentary route it embraced. In a discourse on Spain's attitudes to trade unionism, she pronounced:

There is no doubt that the magnificent struggle of the Spanish workers challenges the entire theory and historical interpretation of parliamentary socialism. The civil war is a living proof of the futility and worthlessness of parliamentary democracy as a medium for social change.

Denouncing the democratic course being pursued by the republican government was a brave move on MacDonald's part, and she soon found herself vilified by the communists and in grave danger of arrest. MacDonald and Patrick's words in the *Barcelona Bulletin* placed both women in peril, and MacDonald aggravated the situation by helping to arm militiamen and women in their Barcelona street fights. After Patrick returned to Scotland on 24 May, MacDonald was forced into hiding, though she continued her work for the anarchist militias, smuggling food and letters to prisoners and assisting the escape from Spain of men wanted by republican authorities. The Bellshill woman's troubles earned her the soubriquet of 'The Scots Scarlet

Pimpernel', though that notoriety came at a cost; MacDonald was eventually captured and imprisoned on several occasions, firstly for failing to renew her residence permit, then, just days after her release, for 'visiting, harbouring, and associating with counter-revolutionary aliens'. MacDonald later described to the *Glasgow Evening Times* how even her first arrest had been politically motivated:

My arrest was typical of the attitude of the Communist Party. In Scotland the group to which I am attached has always been in complete opposition to the Communist Party. In opposing their propaganda we have always had to face and deal with their fundamental ignorance and brutality. In Spain, their approach is the same. Assault Guards and officials of the Public Order entered the house in which I lived late one night. Without any explanation they commenced to go through thoroughly every room and every cupboard in the house. After having discovered that which to them was sufficient to hang me – revolutionary literature etc. – they demanded to see my passport. On this being shown they informed me that I was in Spain illegally, although I entered Spain quite legally.

In prison, MacDonald enjoyed the sense of comradeship among inmates, though she sensed the malevolent influence of Soviet techniques of repression on their incarceration:

The spirit of the comrades in prison is good. Persecution and imprisonment of revolutionists is not something new to Spain. Even persecution by so-called Communists is not new. The treatment meted out to the revolutionists in Russia today beggars description. That can be expected from the present regime in the Socialist fatherland. But that in Spain, whilst their comrades and brothers are struggling at the fronts against the fascist enemy, revolutionists should be arrested on such a scale is a scandal that brings discredit on all those who permit such to take place without making protest. Revolution should mean the end of prisons, not the changing of the guard.

Amazingly, from her cell MacDonald continued to run an information network enabling sustained agitation against republican suppression. She recounted her insurrectionary work in a Christmas 1937 interview given to the *Sunday Mail*:

I used to collect packets of letters from the other prisoners and smuggle them out with my own in the cans in which my food had been brought into prison. Several persons brought in my food but none of them knew they were taking out letters. The cans always landed in the hands of the same man and he knew what to do with them. By means of this channel, too, we managed to organise a hunger strike in every prison in Barcelona in which there were anarchist prisoners. I also spent time arranging how, when one of us got out, we would help the others to flee the country. Everything was cut and dried. Street plans were prepared and everyone knew exactly what to do and where to go.

A pamphlet on Spain produced by one of Glasgow's anarchist splinter groups in support of the CNT-FAI.

MacDonald's eventual release, however, was obtained not by these clandestine activities, but through the intervention of ILP man Fenner Brockway. Despite Brockway's assertion at the time that 'she is an anarchist and has no connection with our party', while on a visit to Spain he visited the Minister of the Interior in Valencia to request that MacDonald be charged and tried or released. Accordingly, on the evening of Thursday 8 July, MacDonald was released from prison.

Brockway advised the now notorious 'Scots Scarlet Pimpernel' to head straight for Britain and safety. Never one to opt for the easy option, she remained in Spain, determined to carry on in her 'effort to serve'. MacDonald then 'disappeared' for several weeks, triggering press speculation in the UK as to her exploits and whereabouts. Her anxious parents made repeated overtures to the British Consulate in Spain for assistance in locating their daughter. The *Glasgow Herald* reported on 2 August that, despite her poverty, MacDonald's mother would 'gladly sell her furniture to raise money to bring her daughter back home if only she could get contact with her.' The MacDonalds' concerns were heightened courtesy of a menacing letter they received from one Helen BS Lennox, speculating that MacDonald could have been struck down by the same forces that she had accused of killing Bob Smillie:

> The Secret Service operating today in Spain comes by night and its victims are never seen again. Bob Smillie they didn't dare to bump off openly, but he may have suffered more because of that. Your Ethel certainly believes his death was intended. She prophesised it before his death took place, and said he would not be allowed out of the country with the knowledge he had. What worries me more than anything is that Ethel has already been ill and would be easy prey for anyone trying to make her death appear natural.

This letter cruelly played upon the fragile state of MacDonald's mother. A self-proclaimed psychic, she duly became convinced of her daughter's death. Mrs MacDonald told the *Sunday Post* that she was convinced Ethel's ghost had visited the family home, confessing, 'As I have gone about my housework this week I have repeatedly fancied I heard a voice calling "Mother".'

Reassurance as to MacDonald's likely wellbeing was contained in an open letter to the Scottish press from David Murray, who suggested that communications from her had been obstructed by the sluggish nature of Spain's wartime infrastructure:

> The friends and parents of Miss MacDonald may reasonably be anxious about her continued non-appearance. They should realise, however, that slow travelling and faulty postal, telegraphic and telephonic communication are normal in Spain.

Further welcome words came from Robert Martin of Stevenston in Ayrshire. Though he had originally travelled to Spain as a potential volunteer with the International Brigades, in Barcelona he had been jailed for being a 'fascist' (after surviving the sinking of ss *Ciudad de Barcelona*, Martin had deserted from the Brigade HQ at Albacete and hidden with POUM comrades in Catalonia). In prison, Martin had formed a lasting friendship with MacDonald, and was able to report, back in Scotland after his escape, of her continued health and freedom 'to walk about the streets as I have here'.

To the relief of MacDonald's friends and relatives, in early August Aldred received a letter from Spain carrying news of her location. After her release on 8 July, she had been re-arrested and imprisoned for a further 12 days. The Scots Scarlet Pimpernel admitted she was now living an undercover, destitute life, sleeping rough and trying to avoid detection and further imprisonment:

> You will have been expecting to hear from me sooner. Due to the usual,

or unusual, unforeseen accidents, that was impossible. Most of the people I knew here left for their respective countries, and sometimes it is pretty lonely. My financial situation is bad. From the clothes aspect, if I am not home soon, it will be too cold to come home at all. I am a terrible sight. All my documents and clothes have gone beyond recall. I have lost everything.

In a further letter to Aldred that week, MacDonald announced that she was now unable to leave Spain lawfully:

I am still here [in Barcelona] and unable to leave the country legally. I am 'in hiding' or living 'illegally'. I cannot get a visa. If I apply I shall be arrested. If I do not apply I shall be arrested. You must help. I would be foolish if I did not know the danger I am now in.

This was not, of course, in accordance with Martin's statement that MacDonald had autonomy over her movements, but, putting that disparity aside, her parents at least had the satisfaction of knowing their daughter was alive. Notwithstanding, these inconsistencies did result in scepticism over MacDonald's plight from other quarters. David Murray wrote a letter informing Guy Aldred that MacDonald could quite easily obtain a police exit visa if she had the motivation to do so, as he had recently fulfilled this task when in Barcelona. Murray had received information that, contrary to scare stories spread by Aldred, MacDonald had remained in Barcelona as 'she likes Spain and I think is in love with a fellow there'. It was Murray's feeling that Aldred had allowed himself to be exploited by the press into validating anti-republican stories surrounding MacDonald that suited their own agenda. Aldred reacted furiously to Murray's accusation that MacDonald 'evidently wants to stay in Spain', and reiterated that he was working hard to secure her passage home. It was his belief that she had been commuted to Valencia and was in grave danger:

I am able to say that Ethel MacDonald left Barcelona mysteriously, and not of her own accord. Valencia is not the way to freedom, but to execution. Her situation is serious, most grave.

MacDonald was to spend a further fortnight in a republican prison in Valencia for her anarchist associations, until finally Aldred was able to ascertain from the British Consulate in that city that she would be released in September before being transported to Nimes, in France, for urgent medical treatment. Never afraid of letting facts get in the way of a good story, the *Daily*

Express ran a piece under the erroneous headline 'Scots girl freed by Franco' on 25 September. MacDonald was finally on her way back to Scotland. Not as gravely ill as Aldred had appeared to believe, she gave speeches in Paris and Amsterdam in aid of the 'Committee for the Aid and Succour of the Victims of the Counter-revolutionary Communist Party Persecution in Spain'. Then on 7 November 1937, the Scots Scarlet Pimpernel was welcomed home to Glasgow by a crowd of 300 people at Central Station. But when MacDonald stepped up to the podium and revealed her disappointment at the capitulation of the Spanish left and its revolution, their ebullience ebbed away:

I went to Spain full of hopes and dreams. It promised to be utopia realised. I return full of sadness, dulled by the tragedy I have seen. I have lived through scenes and events that belong to the French revolution.

MacDonald subsequently toured Scotland giving indicatively entitled lectures such as 'Spain – a Lost Horizon'. She was a scathing and impassioned opponent of the Communist Party and its role in Spain. As so often, in Scotland she found herself arguing against the majority position, but this only served to embolden her. Her tendency to be something of a loose cannon robbed her of potential political allies such as David Murray, who aired his exasperation with her in a letter to Fenner Brockway written shortly after her final release from prison:

She may have had disagreeable experiences but was never in any danger of being 'bumped off'. She also had ample opportunity to leave Spain, where she was performing no useful work for anybody. She entirely neglected to learn Spanish to any degree. Every little bleating message which came from Spain about her was given full publicity in the *Glasgow Evening Times*. She claimed to have special knowledge about Bob Smillie and continued to spread the story that he was done to death.

Certainly, MacDonald's year in Spain had been a controversial and eventful one. As with the case of Bob Smillie, a Scottish story had reflected in microcosm the wider destructive battles raging within the republican left. The legend of the Scots Scarlet Pimpernel represented an intriguing and telling subplot in Scotland's relationship with the Spanish Civil War.

CHAPTER 14

Last Heroic Acts:
Aragon and the Ebro

*I simply cannot describe in words how keen I feel about my participation
in the war, actually in the Battalion with which I will soon be in the
front line. This is no mere propaganda splash, I never felt just quite so
enthusiastic about anything as I am about this great struggle. We are
going to win – yes we are and that without undue delay.*
Tom Murray

AWAY FROM THE politicking surrounding Bob Smillie and Ethel MacDonald,
in the summer of 1937 hundreds of Scots remained in Spain, their version of
the country far removed from tit-for-tat newspaper allegations and rumours
of wrongdoing. Despite their demoralising defeat at Brunete, the British
Battalion vowed to regroup and fight on. Their resolve to continue amounted
to a clarion call: the Battalion was in Spain to fight until it was told it no
longer could.

In August, the Battalion moved into the Aragon region of northeast Spain
ahead of a planned republican assault on the nationalist-held town of Quinto.
Morale had begun to rise again, and the Battalion leaders felt their men were
now equipped to launch an attack. Machine-gun company commander Robert
Walker, son of the great Hearts player Bobby, reassured Peter Kerrigan:

> You don't need to worry about the Brigade now. It's improved beyond
> recognition and the Brigade leadership characterises our Battalion as
> the best in the Brigade. The spirit is grand and this is reflected in the
> efficiency of the military work.

Walker was proved right when the Battalion helped rout the nationalists
in Quinto. The town was captured within two days of the launch of their
offensive. Heartened by this success, the republicans moved on to Fuentes
de Ebro, a town beside the strategically vital River Ebro, with the aim of
seizing it and moving into the surrounding valley ahead of an advance on
Zaragoza. It was an objective they fell catastrophically short of completing,
their heavy and unsophisticated reliance on tank attacks reaping very little
reward. Runner Hugh Sloan, a Fife miner, labelled the advance a 'ridiculous

charge like that of the Light Brigade – a gallant effort but a stupid effort.'[26]

Regardless of their calamitous experience at Fuentes de Ebro, the British contingent of the republican army pressed on to Belchite, emerging victorious from a traumatic rash of hand-to-hand combat with the nationalists. Hugh Sloan recalled the unique nature of combat at Belchite:

Belchite was a particular kind of battle at close quarters. You were seeing the person you were killing. That's a different thing from killing people at a distance. In that respect it was a very bitter battle.

With this intense fighting came scenes as horrific as any in this most bloody of wars, as Sloan continued:

I remember walking up what you could call the main street, and I couldn't bear the smell of death. Some of our people were digging large holes into which all sorts of remains of living things, humans but also pigs and goats, were being thrown. We came to the square. There was a very large heap of dead human beings piled up. And in the very hot weather the smell was completely unbearable.

Members of the Anti-tank Battery pause for a photograph in the searing Aragon sun in August 1937. Scots Bill Cranston, Hugh Sloan and Chris Smith (bottom row, left) sit together, with Arthur Nicoll perched just behind them.

The Battalion's greatest success in Aragon was to come on 8 January 1938, when they played a key part in capturing the town of Teruel. After this spirited victory, the mood among Brigaders improved greatly, and celebratory parties were held. John Ross felt that the triumphs in Aragon had bred a new-found sense of unity on the republican side, as he wrote on 30 January:

The different armies of the unions, anarchists, etc., are now united in a single People's Army, well-trained, well-disciplined, under a capable general staff purged of the elements which were a main cause of the defeats and unwise retreats last year. The effectiveness of this new army is proved

by the magnificent victory of Teruel, taken with amazingly small losses according to schedule and held ever since against the terrific counter-attacks which have lost Franco thousands of men.

The gains of Aragon had escalated the feeling within the Battalion that republican success was now inevitable, as Ross enthusiastically continued:

With this improved organisation in the rearguard and the whole Spanish people on our side, there is no doubt about our ultimate victory. Everybody is impatient to go to the front and the morale of the men is magnificent. Against such volunteers, fighting for convictions, side by side with Spaniards fighting for their life and liberty, the forces of Franco have no chance.

Sadly, this optimism soon ebbed away as the British Battalion were forced, from the end of January, into

Archie Dewar (back, left) poses with Glaswegian and Spanish comrades in happier times; he was to die during the retreat from Aragon.

a series of retreats amidst a fierce nationalist onslaught. That month had begun happily for the British, with buoyancy surrounding the victory of Teruel allied to first anniversary celebrations of the Battalion's debut at the Jarama. As Garry Mc-Cartney recalled, the birthday was marked in a very patriotic way, the men 'stuffing away double rations of bacon and eggs with real English tea'. Yet celebration soon turned to commiseration, as Franco's forces powered into Teruel and forced the republicans to decamp some 70 miles over the following days, brutally taking back Belchite as they did so. Brave stands were made at Caspe and Batea, as the British Battalion attempted to stunt the nationalist advance towards Spain's east coast. However, they were eventually forced back to Calaceite, where at the end of March over 100 were ambushed and imprisoned, as docu-

The bell tower at Belchite where Barney Shields held out, the last republican in the area.

mented above. The Battalion, now just 80-strong, retreated to Gandesa, before the nationalists pushed them out, and back over the River Ebro where a retreat of 125 miles finally came to a halt.

Scottish Brigaders played a central, by parts heroic and harrowing, role in the fighting in Aragon. During the siege of Belchite, as the republicans strove to hold on to the town and arrest their retreat, Barney Shields took up position in the bell tower of a Catholic cathedral, with only his machine-gun for company. Besieged by nationalist troops, Shields' republican commander demanded an immediate flight from the area. Shields, though, took it upon himself to remain in the bell tower picking out nationalist troops until finally, as the only republican left in the area, he was flushed out and brutally killed.

In the retreat from Belchite, Robert Walker was one of four Brigaders who unwittingly walked into the middle of a nationalist patrol. The four men were instructed at gunpoint to drop their weapons and place their hands in the air. Surprisingly, Franco's troops concerned themselves not with carting them off as valuable prisoners, but instead looted their pockets for money and their wrists for watches. As the captors placed their guns on the floor to indulge in this bout of larceny, Walker whispered to his comrades 'now's our chance' and landed an almighty blow to the face of his own personal thief. Walker's comrades, Sam Wild and Joe Norman, quickly got in on the act, booting a further two soldiers to the floor. Meanwhile, the fourth member of the quartet, Harry Dobson, added a touch of the slapstick to proceedings, grabbing a tin of 'bully beef' from his bag and knocking a final man out cold. The four sprinted away into the darkness and rough terrain of the Aragon countryside, grateful for their spare portion of processed meat.

Looting and food featured, too, in the exploits of Dundonian Brigaders Malcolm Smith, whom John Dunlop described as having 'the strong red face of an Angus farmer', and Micky Sullivan. The two were among those who had escaped capture at Calaceite, but soon found themselves detached from their fellow escapees and ensconced in nationalist territory. Upon hearing the whir of an approaching tank, Smith and Sullivan dived for cover, anticipating the arrival of a battalion. They were relieved to see, instead, a solitary tank, which Smith and Sullivan instinctively fired upon with their Soviet-supplied Dikterov machine-gun. The armoured vehicle burst into flames, at which point its crewmembers spilled onto the road. They were met with another burst of Smith and Sullivan's fire, and swiftly killed. The happy result for the two Brigaders was the chance to ransack the tank for its contents, which turned out to consist of generous food supplies. The starving men gratefully enjoyed their finest meal in months while seated upon a tank marked with fascist insignia, and then found their way back into friendly territory.

With Franco's German and Italian troops attacking incisively and brutally, such tales of glee were predictably rare during the Aragon retreat. Alec Park described the devastation left by nationalist soldiers as they passed through the region:

> I was in a village where the fascist bombers a few days ago had given to the inhabitants just exactly what is meant to represent the new fascist culture which is to save the whole world from Red Ruin. The scene of destruction is indescribable but the horror of it all is written in the faces of the women.

That horror was not reserved for the natives. According to a number of Brigaders, nationalist forces employed expanding 'dum-dum' bullets during the retreat, a violation of the Geneva Convention. Steve Fullarton witnessed the impact of this weaponry on George Kelly of Greenock, remembering that "his forearm from the wrist to the elbow was just a gaping hole". Similarly terrifying was the ordeal suffered by Glaswegian David Stirrat, who became separated from the rest of the British Battalion. As they withdrew across the River Ebro, he and a small band of other volunteers were left over the line. In a letter to his father written on 20 April, Stirrat gave a detailed account of their efforts to avoid detection and get back to their comrades:

Ruined houses at Belchite

I was a machine-gunner and we were the Company who bumped into the enemy tanks first. We were about a hundred yards from the first tank when it opened fire on us and we got our gun mounted and hit them back. Then the first tanks burst into flames and we kept the other back for about two hours until we found that the machine-gun company (by that time about 30 men) had been cut off from the rest. Well there was only five of us got out of that and it took me and another chap eighteen days to do it. We took to the mountains and followed the fascist advance from day to day. Several times we tried to get through their front line but we could never manage it. I think if it had not been for the thought of my mother I would have given up trying, because we didn't have much chance then and the grub wasn't too plentiful. As the days went by we got used to things a bit and began to find more food by 'various methods'. Then about ten days later we struck the River Ebro and discovered that it was the enemy flank so we decided to have a go at swimming over.

We met an American then and tried the river two nights later but it was too strong at that point and the American drowned because he was a poor swimmer. We got back again to fascist territory and met two Germans in a house where there was plenty flour and olive oil and we 'found' nine rabbits so after a few days when the grub was finished we decided to have another go at the river. We tried it at a different place and swam over at night. We all got over to within a few feet of this bank and were standing in the river shaking hands when one of the Germans spoke out loud and our own guards started firing at us, chucked a hand grenade, it was like a bloomin' fireworks night. Three of us made a dive for the bank but the other German got the wind up and buzzed off back to the other side again. They took us prisoner and when they discovered who we were they treated us well. Well I have lost everything but my mind. I think I've lost half of that so maybe you would send me a cheap shaving kit.

Safely returned to the republicans, though suffering terrible illness, Stirrat was able to impart his knowledge of nationalist territory to his military commanders, thus playing a fundamental part in what was to become perhaps the greatest accomplishment of the British Battalion in Spain: the crossing of the River Ebro.

By the summer of 1938, Franco's army was advancing rapidly on Madrid, which was something of a republican stronghold. As they moved eastwards towards Valencia, it became clear that the nationalists intended to encircle the Spanish capital. The response of the republican high command was to instigate an audacious raid back southwards over the River Ebro and into nationalist territory.

On 21 July the British Battalion were informed that they would be among an army of 80,000 republicans undertaking this forward surge. Their own aim was to assist in capturing the town of Gandesa, a strategically important settlement in the southwest of Catalonia. Over the subsequent days, Battalion members were divided into groups and transported by truck towards the banks of the Ebro. The final leg of their journey was to be completed on foot, though for some of the men this proved to be a somewhat trying task, as Tom Murray later recollected:

> We were marching up a road during the night. Suddenly a blooming bomb went off, and this was Eddie Brown, who was overloaded with belts of ammunition, carrying a light machine-gun on his shoulder, and he had several hand grenades laced on his belt. He had laced one of them by the loop of the safety pin, and walking up there the blooming thing came out and dropped down and exploded. There were about 13 men injured. I was coming up a good distance back, then came this explosion. Some of them came running down and I says, 'fascists? We're at the wrong side of the Ebro for the fascists. It's some of our own people. It's a load of nonsense. There's been an accident of some kind.' But Eddie Brown walked on, he walked straight on, and this blooming thing was sizzling behind him and he was clear of the danger.[27]

Brown, Murray and their comrades lived to later laugh at the incident, though it had been a close call. On 25 July, republican troops began their mass-crossing of the Ebro on a fleet of small boats organised by the American Lincoln-

Members of the British Battalion offer a defiant salute at Marsa one month ahead of their participation in the crossing of the River Ebro. They are led by Bob Cooney of Aberdeen, now Battalion Commissar.

Washington Battalion. As the soldiers moved stealthily towards the boats, they came under a barrage of fire from above. John Dunlop explained:

> By the time we got down, the crossing was in full swing. We came down towards the Ebro through a dry watercourse with thick reed beds alongside it. We kept in close to the reed beds because we were under constant attack from one or two enemy aircraft. They were huge silver beasts and they were swooping down and machine-gunning anywhere they thought we might be.[28]

Despite this peril, the crossing of the Ebro was a monumental success. The precision and professionalism of the operation reflected the fact that Spain's republican army, still with a large quotient of volunteer members, had come of age. That the British Battalion had played a part in the crossing and indeed in that coming of age made it all the sweeter for men like Eddie Brown, John Dunlop and Tom Murray. Also present at the Ebro was George Murray, who became convinced that the crossing represented a watershed in the war. He announced in a letter home:

> The effect of our advance over the Ebro should be great for it certainly constitutes one of the biggest smashes in the eye that Mussolini and

his company ever got and proves the vitality and capacity of the truly magnificent Spanish people. Two years of bitter front line fighting and wanton slaughter in the rear by Italian–German aviation have failed to destroy not only their spirit but also their resourcefulness and initiative.

His brother Tom was similarly glowing:

We have had the glorious privilege of participating in the remarkable victory of the crossing of the Ebro. I am sitting on a hill about 20 kilometres inside what was until a fortnight ago fascist territory. You may take it that the advance we have made is merely a prelude of more to come, although of course we are well aware that fascism will throw still more materiel and men into the struggle in the hope that by doing so this position will be retrieved. We have no illusions that the victory will be an easy one but on the other hand the recent success confirms with tremendous emphasis the power of the Spanish Republic and sends the morale of all lovers of freedom and justice shooting up to great heights.

An air of optimism now pervaded the British Battalion, though they had very little time to ruminate for too long on their achievements; from the moment the first crossers stepped onto the north bank of the Ebro, the nationalists unleashed an almighty volley of gunfire upon them. Steve Fullarton sketched out the chaotic, darkly comic scenes that ensued:

On arrival we came under fire and one of our number was wounded in the foot. He started calling for the enfermo but it was difficult to reach him without risk, when our sergeant called to him to 'be quiet or you will give your position away', the wounded man called back: 'Well, if I haven't already given my position away, then some bastard must've told them where I am.'

A day after their safe passage over the Ebro, the Battalion were back in offensive action as part of the republican section attempting to capture Hill 481, adjacent to Gandesa. Here they became stymied by a determined nationalist defensive operation and British casualties in particular quickly mounted during six days of intensive fighting in the mainland summer swelter of Spain. Dunlop spoke of the ill-fated storming of 481:

I can't remember how many days we spent on the opposing hillside. We had to keep down below the skyline during the day. We were attacking across the valley and up the hill on the other side. Their position was very well defended and our attacks were continually being broken up not so much by fire that they were raining on us but the whole place was littered with grenades and trip wires in the undergrowth. I remember one occasion like that when these explosions started up. I threw myself on the ground and I was lifted bodily by the explosion of a grenade just a few feet in front of my nose. I was extremely lucky that I got no other damage apart from some scratches to my legs and ankles. It really was a hellish place to be. I think that was just about the time when I felt the lowest in all my life.

As well as facing danger when on manoeuvres, at Hill 481 Brigaders were afflicted by the constant menace of nationalist fire even when static. Having been wounded and hospitalised, Steve Fullarton wrote from his sickbed with a description of nightly events:

Steady fighting was carried on all the time. Each night there would be some fun. The fascists would think they saw or heard something and fire at it. Then someone else would fire where the shot came from. The machine-guns would open up, then the trench mortars, then the artillery, all over nothing. Sometimes it would happen two or three times in one night, usually lasting one hour.

The action frequently took a less remote course; Fullarton continued with an account of the paralysing personal and collective effects of fierce hill-to-hill combat:

As the battle calmed down, I got up to our lieutenant who had been wounded with shrapnel in the leg and a bullet through the arm. I put a tourniquet on his arm and he told me to find cover until dark and then get him back to our position. I saw a shell hole close by and was just getting into it when I got it in the stomach. Things were quietening down now and many were calling for the 'sanituro' and their 'madre'. The fascists were answering them and kidding them, if not by mouth with machine-guns. When I saw this was happening, after I got hit I lay still and kept quiet so as not to give my position away. While I lay there waiting for darkness to come I kept alert in case the Moors would come out to bayonet the wounded.

Convinced he would not last the night, Fullarton pulled the pins from his final two grenades, 'one for them, and one for me – I preferred it that way rather than let them get me.' Somehow, though, he managed to stay conscious and crawl his way back to company base. 'The bullet made an ugly hole,' he wrote from hospital, 'but I will soon be OK again.'

Fullarton was one of the lucky ones. Tom Murray was witness to the appalling after effects of an incident in which three Scottish Brigaders were pummelled by a round of anti-tank fire:

> I found George Jackson lying stretched out. George came from Cowdenbeath and I think he was one of the recruits that I got to go with me when I went out there. Charlie McLeod of Aberdeen was lying with his head on George Jackson's chest. And Malcolm Smith was lying about a yard or so away. All were dead by the blast of this anti-tank shell.[29]

In their grief, Charlie McLeod's family contacted Murray demonstrating typical support for the cause: 'We are proud of our son and brother, he gave his life for what he believed in. We only hope his sacrifice was not in vain.' Murray replied in stirring terms, stating that McLeod was one of many Brigaders who had left him emboldened rather than deflated by what he had witnessed. He declared:

> I returned from Spain feeling that I had seen demonstrated the finest qualities that human beings possess, and have more respect than ever for the majesty of the human being.

In spite of the hardships faced, morale among the members of the British Battalion remained fairly high in this, their final summer in Spain. Prior to his hospitalisation, Steve Fullarton had enjoyed aspects of his time next to and around the River Ebro. There, strength and even joy were knitted out of adversity. In 2008, he was still particularly proud of the bivouacs (named 'Chabolas' after their location) he and his fellow Scottish Brigaders constructed ahead of their crossing the river:

> We stopped at Chabola Valley. When we were told we'd be staying there for a few days, Dusty Miller wasted no time in cutting down a tree to make a Chabola. He cut this tree down and made a Chabola with the leaves and the earth: I've an idea that it's still there yet, still existing, because it was 'Clyde Built', more or less.

It was in this Chabola community that Fullarton's friend Jimmy Glavin, of Govan, caused a stir when dispatched to collect supplies:

At night time before we went to the Ebro, we used to have a fire and singsong at that place. They would get a big jar of wine from the village at the end – Torre de Fontana Bella – so somebody would have to go for it and a bag of nuts, hazelnuts. It came to Jimmy's turn to go into the village one night with somebody else. Jimmy and the other man, off they went to the village. They took a long time to get back, we were getting anxious about them. Eventually he came back, drunk as can be. Somebody got on to him, 'Where have you been?' 'I've been in the village for wine and nuts.' By this time, we'd picked up the jar. 'You've been drinking it!' 'Well,' he said, 'it was heavy!'

As the campaign at Hill 481 continued, such revelry receded as the besieged British Battalion were forced backwards, eventually settling on 1 August at the ominously-named Hill 666, on the Sierra Pandols mountain range. There, they were put into reserve, and could do nothing about a nationalist onslaught that finally put paid to any remaining hopes the republican army had of capturing Gandesa. On 24 August, the British relieved the fatigued Abraham Lincoln Battalion in action on 666, which proved to be another ruinous sweep of engagements with the enemy. On 9 September, the Battalion was transferred to Hill 356, close to Sandesco, which, incredibly, given the decimation in the ranks, it managed to capture. In a letter to his wife Janet, Tom Murray detailed the surroundings in which the British found themselves at Hill 666, though his words were applicable to all three of the battle mounds they operated on in this period:

It may interest you if I mention some of the things seen, heard and felt by me as I sit on this hilltop. First of all, the noise. Machine-guns with incessant rattle, the monotonous rattle of avion, deafening explosions, some close by and some distant, or aerial bombs, the sharp explosion of trench mortar bombs and the terrific explosions of heavy artillery shells, the whole racket becoming a blend. The area is pitted with shell holes. Along to my immediate left is the new grave of an English comrade we buried this

Tom Murray, Labour Councillor in Edinburgh, Commissar of the British Battalion's machine-gun company in Spain, pauses pensively amidst the 'monotonous rattle of avion' at Hill 666.

morning. To my right a group of comrades are calmly opening fish and meat tins for their midday meals, laughing and joking in the most normal manner, though well aware of the most exceptional circumstances in which they are located. In a little valley in front of me lie three wounded comrades on stretchers awaiting evacuation to the clearing station at the foot of the hill. They require water and we gladly part with our meagre supply for their succour. Wafted up from no-man's-land is the stench from the bodies of dead fascists.

Though the Battalion's tenure on Hill 666 was largely a defensive one, they did launch one injurious assault upon the nationalists, as John Dunlop recalled:

We made this disastrous night attack and we were driven back. It was just because we didn't know what the devil we were supposed to be doing. There wasn't a sufficient preparation for the thing beforehand. The bombs started exploding all around us and it was a bewildering experience.

Dunlop felt that this was the moment when the nationalists' superior military training and equipment proved decisive. The ravaged British Battalion could do very little against the technologically advanced German weaponry.

Their subsequent victory at Sandesco on 7 September represented an astonishing triumph of will. With renewed confidence the Battalion, or what remained of it, moved on to replace the desolated Polish Dombrowski Brigade at nearby Sierra Lavall de la Torre. In the third week of September, as the soldiers of the Battalion anxiously awaited directives on what their role was to be, news filtered through that republican prime minister Juan Negrin had announced to the League of Nations that all foreign volunteers in the Spanish army were to be withdrawn. His hope was that the League would accordingly pressurise Franco, Hitler and Mussolini into similar action.

At Sierra Lavall, the British Battalion were asked to perform one final task a day after Negrin's proclamation of 21 September, as Tommy Bloomfield explained:

When the Battalion was withdrawn from the Ebro for repatriation, Sam Wild paraded us and called for volunteers to go back up to the fighting line for 48 hours to give the republican forces time to bring up fresh troops. Needless to say, all the lads went back in. That was a hard decision to make knowing it meant you could die instead of going home.

The Battalion was overpowered at Sierra Lavall, and many of Bloomfield's comrades were never to make that trip home, the tragedy of their deaths magnified by the fact that they were in touching distance of peace and safety. The men were placed in a location that invited swaths of lethal crossfire, and their trenches were eventually overrun, though many Brigaders remained in place to the last. Over the three days of fighting around the time of Negrin's announcement, more than 200 members of the British Battalion were killed, wounded or reported missing. It was a brutally sour note with which to go out on for this most intrepid of Battalions. After a gallant and dogged resistance, the Spanish-only republican army was subsequently pushed backwards towards Madrid, and their eventual defeat began to appear inevitable. The optimism of the days following the crossing of the Ebro seemed a very distant memory indeed.

CHAPTER 15

Far from Perfect?
Criticism and Dissent

*I can say from personal knowledge and experience that any member
of the Brigade who was unaware that the International Brigades had
been organised by the comintern and were Communist-directed from
beginning to end must have been singularly unperceptive.*
Hamish Fraser, Saltcoats

WHETHER IN CONTEMPORARY allegations made by the Independent Labour
Party and United Socialist Movement, or in post-conflict analyses, questions
have been raised over the popular image of the International Brigades as heroic
and innocent defenders of democracy and freedom. Central to this is the level
of influence upon the Brigades of the Soviet Union; the ILP, USM and many
others have portrayed the Brigades as a mere army of the comintern, their
every move dictated by Moscow. Indeed, it was a decree by the comintern on
26 July 1936 that led to the formation of the Brigades. Additionally, the Soviet
supply of materiel did buy Moscow substantial sway upon Spain's republican
administration, and through its hold on the Brigades the Communist Party
was able to achieve a level of importance it did not possess at the start of the
war.

What could be perceived as manifestations of this influence were detectable
in the undertakings of several Scottish Brigaders, though most of them were
already committed communists before travelling to Spain; that is, their stated
beliefs were not the slavish responses of Muscovite puppets, but rather the
independent conclusions drawn by intelligent men. If anything, the influence
of Moscow on Scottish Brigaders was greater *before* they arrived in Spain.
Indeed six volunteers (George Aitken, Bob Cooney, Thomas Duncan, James
Hyndman, Peter Kerrigan and James Marshall) had, between 1926 and 1937,
attended the prestigious Lenin School in the city, and three of the men were to
become political commissars in Spain.

Once in Spain, Brigaders frequently espoused positive opinions of the
USSR, though again, these were usually views they carried with them from
Scotland rather than adopted under pressure once abroad. There was, too, a
clearly pro-Soviet, or at least anti-POUM, groundswell of opinion following
the disturbances in Barcelona of May 1937.

Tom Murray, who labelled the USSR 'the greatest friend of the Spanish people', referred to the POUM as 'provocateurs' guilty of 'nefarious intrigues and treasonable conduct.' Peter Kerrigan was outraged when he caught wind of a rumour that POUM figures involved in the Barcelona fighting would be exonerated, writing to Harry Pollitt: 'I have found that there is a likelihood of them being tried in secret with a view to the acquittal of the accused. I cannot believe it and am pursuing the matter.'

This ire was extended to the ILP, who were viewed as accessories to the crimes of the POUM. Maryhill Brigader Walter Gregory summarised the thoughts of many Brigaders when he wrote to Kerrigan that 'the only actions the ILP ever did was to engineer along with the POUM the rising in our rear at Barcelona.' It is difficult to argue that Communist Brigaders were not swayed in their views on this issue by the official Party line.

While it is impossible to categorically state where the germination of pro-Soviet views occurred, the influence of Moscow on other facets of the Brigade was more tangible. This is especially true in the case of military discipline, which was perceptibly tightened at the behest of the Communist Party. Two Scots with roles in this increased discipline were Hamish Fraser and George Murray, both of whom were made Battalion SIM representatives charged with what Murray called 'guarding against the insertion of enemy agents.' Anecdotally, in their letters, Scottish volunteers referred to the more rigorous approach applied to Brigade discipline as the war progressed. This was undoubtedly necessitated in part by the early strains placed on the largely inexperienced republican army and their realisation that the war was to be a drawn-out affair. Equally, it does appear that much of this new-found orderliness emanated from Soviet input and instruction. In a December 1937 letter to Peter Kerrigan, Thomas McWhirter remarked with praise on the contribution of the Communist Party, which, whether Spanish or British as here, followed strictly Soviet lines:

> The rapid growth of our army is really marvellous. We are a real fighting force, our Communist Party takes the fullest credit for the way it has fought against all distortions and has welded the Popular Army of the people. No more our slovenly methods of training and general attitude to discipline, we found our methods on true discipline and methods of training that would do credit to any imperialist army.

This clampdown did not impact upon the military sphere alone. Peter Kerrigan remarked that from February 1938 there was a 'much stricter control of the activities' previously designated by Political Commissars, such as wall newspapers and leisure-time events. There also developed a climate of censorship, as Kerrigan highlighted when referring to the *Book of the XVth Brigade*:

The book has now been completed and is being printed off. New regulations however make it necessary to pass a censor and it will have to get his consent before being issued. I don't think there will be any trouble but it's difficult to tell these days.

It would be naïve in the extreme to suggest that the USSR's role on the International Brigades was insignificant; clearly, once they had offered military assistance they expected a level of ideological and strategic control in return (as well as the transfer of Spain's gold reserves). This should not, however, detract from the credibility of the 35,000 people from around the world who travelled to Spain of their own volition, including the Scottish contingent. Many were Communist Party members who already idolised the Soviet Union before going to Spain. Some were communists believing in their own 'Clyde Built' version of the doctrine. Many more were not communists at all. What all these groups had in common was a shared sense of purpose: the defeat of Franco and his fascist allies. No amount of interpretation and reinterpretation can disguise the bare fact that they were neither stooges nor fools.

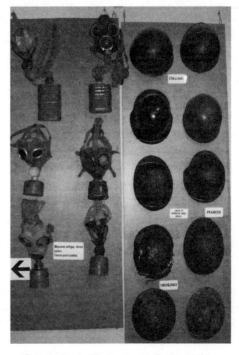

Though the desertion rate in the British Battalion was admirably low (indeed John Dunlop remarked that a greater problem arose from volunteers deserting hospital to travel back to the front line), there were enough cases to suggest that life was not always harmonious. From the middle of 1937 onwards, there was very little chance of the 'six months and then home' that would-be volunteers had previously been assured of; the xvth International Brigade was now formally incorporated into the republican army, meaning shared terms and conditions. Active service would end only when the war did, a

Gas masks and helmets on display at the Spanish Civil War museum at Morata de Tajuña.

Memorial to the International Brigades at Morata de Tajuña.

realisation that prompted an increase in defections from the Battalion.

Perhaps the most infamous Scottish incident was that of the so-called 'Round Robin Deserters', which occurred before the abolition of a national maximum term of service. On 22 March 1937, the ever-supportive *Daily Mail* professed that Brigaders Charlie Craig, Angus MacDonald and John Parker had deserted at the Jarama front due to the high number of Scottish casualties suffered there. To escape, MacDonald had lain prone on a stretcher while the other two stole Red Cross armbands and acted as bearers. Now back in Britain, they had with them a petition signed by more than 30 Brigaders demanding repatriation, which they duly handed over to the Foreign Office. The *Mail* article once more alleged that those who had volunteered to fight in Spain had done so either unknowingly or for large sums of money.

The article and the actions of the three men were met with incandescent fury by the Brigaders who remained in Spain. Bill Gilmour led the assault, writing:

I don't have to tell you that I left a good comfortable home to come out here. I am well led, and have enough pay to meet my needs. We were not compelled to fight. The deserters were all yellow. They ran away while the fight was at its worst. There is some excuse for men whose nerves go under the strain. But there is no punishment severe enough for men who desert their comrades in the thick of the fight, and then go home to GB pertaining to be the bearers of a petition bearing the names of 32 men of our own comrades who wanted to go home.

The remaining members of the British Battalion issued a statement in March 1937 to further quash the claims of the *Mail* and the Round Robin Three:

> We desire it to be known in Britain that we came here of our own free will after full consideration of all that this step involved. We came to Spain not for money, but solely to assist the heroic Spanish people to defend their country's freedom and democracy. We were not gulled into coming to Spain by promises of big money. We never even asked for money when we volunteered. We are perfectly satisfied with our treatment by the Spanish government; and we still are proud to be fighting for the cause of freedom. Any statements to the contrary are foul lies.

A backlash occurred in Scotland; while queuing to collect his income support money in Dundee, John Parker was badly beaten for what locals saw as his betrayal of working class solidarity with republican Spain. In the longer term, the continued raft of Scottish volunteers and ongoing existence of the British Battalion suggested the Round Robin Deserters' claims had been wide of the mark. A slow drip of further runaways did, however, persist. As a political commissar, Bob Cooney was charged with questioning two Brigaders who had been caught while trying to desert, namely Pat Glacken of Greenock, and Alex Kemp of Glasgow. According to his findings, Kemp had sold the idea of deserting to Glacken, and the two had attempted to cross over to the nationalists. Their motives for doing so remained unclear. A tribunal, which Cooney did not sit on, decided their fate: Glacken was allowed to rejoin the Brigades as a baker, while Kemp became the only man in the history of the British Battalion to be executed by firing squad, as Cooney explained:

> Kemp was shot by firing squad, but not for desertion. He was shot because in order to carry out his desertion he was prepared to betray the lives of his comrades by giving information to the fascists. None of the lads relished the job of carrying out the execution but at the same time they could all have been wiped out because of the actions of Kemp and Glacken.[30]

This was a particularly rare punishment for a particularly rare crime; Battalion justice for smaller offences amounted to Cooney's philosophy of 'you would speak with a lad to talk things over', while for desertion, Alec Park insightfully described the usual procedure, penalty and reasoning therein:

Friday afternoon is usually the Battalion political meeting but last Friday instead of the customary meeting the platform was occupied by a military tribunal and an individual charged with desertion, tried and sentenced. The men formed the jury, put questions and finally pronounced the verdict. Everything in connection with the accused was brought before the court; his social and political affiliations in civil life, his conduct since coming from Spain and even his recent correspondence with home. The prosecution brought out, to my mind a very strong point, and that is that before he could have left republican Spain some assistance would be necessary. Such assistance would only be rendered by anti-government and fascist forces within. Such an individual would in all probability get immense publicity in the capitalist and fascist press of the world. The only answer to which is that the men here are all keen to come to grips with the fascists and that one deserter does not in any way represent the outlook of the foreign anti-fascist forces in Spain. The verdict of the court was duly pronounced and although the extreme penalty could have been inflicted, he was given such a sentence as will enable him to rehabilitate himself with his comrades.

While Park's words represent a description of 'in-house' justice at the front line, deserters who managed to escape the Battalion often found themselves indefinitely imprisoned. The republican authorities were far less lenient than their comrades in the highest echelons of the British Battalion. Crieff Brigader John Gordon arrived in Spain in December 1937, but recoiled from the reality of war. Having deserted, he was captured and spent several months in Valencia's Model Prison, before eventually being repatriated in April 1938. Having been wounded at Calaceite, Dundee-born Henry Burns absconded from Moya hospital only to be captured and imprisoned at Casteldefels, an International Brigades jail close to Tarragona. Unlike Gordon, rather than being deported Burns was escorted back to the British Battalion, where he failed to find favour; a subsequent CPGB evaluation of Burns read 'Bad, drunkard, deserter, disrupter.'

Though ex-members of the British Battalion rather than ILP men, David Murray willingly visited and assisted James Donald, John Mudie and Malcolm Sneddon, all imprisoned in Valencia's Model Prison on charges of desertion. Donald and Mudie were arrested on 25 February 1937, having made their way to Valencia with the help of drivers similar to those used by the escapee cohorts of Captain Edwin Lance, while Sneddon had earlier been detained on similar charges.

Murray provided much-needed assistance for all three men, writing to their relatives and supplying them with cigarettes, clothing, underwear and money. Back in Methil, news of James Donald's wellbeing was particularly appreciated by his family, who had been wrongly informed of his death. While Donald's stretch was his first and only, Dundonian John Mudie spent most of his time in Spain in penal and medical institutions. Murray described finding Mudie in extremely poor fettle on one particular occasion:

He had no shirt and had no money since his arrival in Spain, was badly fed (a hunger strike on the part of the anti-fascists resulted in still worse food, fit 'for a pig'), and had refused to go into line.

In June, Mudie was dispatched to a prison in Alicante, where he spent three months before being made to work as a guard at a Hospital in Villa Paz. Unfortunately, Mudie was soon removed from this position for drunkenness, before winding up in hospital with VD. He was later to serve and die in Aragon, a dramatic end to a dramatic Spanish sojourn.

Rather than an indictment of the International Brigades, these desertions were reflections on the personalities and circumstances of individuals. While there were a few seemingly incorrigible men like Mudie, many simply failed to grasp the horrors service in Spain would bring. Writing home to Glasgow, Brigader George Gilmour displayed an attitude towards desertion common among his fellow volunteers, and also depicted the overall spirit of defiance that, sometimes surprisingly, permeated the British Battalion throughout its existence:

I hear that a man named [censored] has made his way home from Alicante. It is being reported that he is telling wives of good comrades that they should plead that they have divers disease and invent all the excuses they have to get their husbands home. This man is a deserter – a yellow renegade. What is the real spirit in our ranks? Let me give you an example. Over a fortnight ago a barrage started as the fascists were attempting to break through on our left flank. The rain had been pouring down all day, and all through the barrage, which started at night, it poured. Along the trenches, above the din of machine-gun fire, rifle and artillery fire, could be heard the strains of the 'Internationale', 'Tipperary' and the 'Red Flag'; and all the folk tunes and popular melodies we could think of were sung that night in good community style, in spite of the fact that we were knee deep in water and soaked to the skin.

A more serious threat to the morale of the British Battalion and the reputation of the International Brigades came during the summer of 1937, when two leading Scottish figures in Spain became embroiled in a furious spree of in-fighting. The dispute began when Battalion political commissar Walter Tapsell claimed that the promotions of Scots George Aitken (to Brigade Commissar) and Jock Cunningham (to Battalion commander) had left the two men isolated from regular Brigaders. Tapsell wrote that, 'Aitken's temperament has made him distrusted and disliked by the vast majority of the British Battalion who regard him as being personally ambitious and unmindful of the interests of the Battalion and the men.' Meanwhile, Cunningham, 'fluctuates violently between hysterical bursts of passion and is openly accused by Aitken of lazing about the Brigade headquarters doing nothing.' Assistant Brigade Commissar at Albacete, Dave Springhall, weighed in, claiming that the Battalion's entire leadership structure had collapsed under the pressures brought on by defeat at Brunete.

With an amicable resolution impossible in Spain, all parties involved were summoned back to London for a meeting with CPGB leader Harry Pollitt. At its conclusion, Pollitt told Aitken, Cunningham and Bert Williams (a political commissar with the Abraham Lincoln Battalion) to remain in Britain, while Fred Copeman (commander of the British Battalion) and Tapsell were to return to Spain. Aitken and Cunningham, though barely on speaking terms themselves, were apoplectic at the decision, and the former wrote a 10-page letter of 'emphatic protest' to the CPGB, in response to 'this monstrous injustice'.

Within a matter of months, both had resigned from the Party, and the leadership of the British Battalion had been radically reshaped. As part of its restructuring, the Battalion became an official part of the republican army, meaning popular six month terms of service were now prohibited. Disputes at the top of the hierarchy had undermined soldier morale and damaged the reputation of the Brigades on a level that the smattering of desertions at the bottom never could.

CHAPTER 16

The Unbitter End:
Going Home and Being Home

Led proudly by their wounded comrades, the men marched through London. With them marched the spirit of Byron, the Tolpuddle Martyrs, the Chartists and Keir Hardie, Britain's bravest fighters for liberty through the centuries. Behind them and around them marched twenty thousand British democrats.

Report, *London Star*

JUAN NEGRIN'S PROCLAMATION that foreign volunteers were to be withdrawn from Spain with near-immediate effect came as something of a surprise to Brigaders on the front line. Many were instantaneously aggrieved that they would now be unable to complete the job as intended. Gratitude for that which they had achieved was expressed in a final parade through Barcelona on 28 October 1938. Thirteen thousand International Brigaders marched across the Catalan capital, their passage made sluggish as they received the personal and heartfelt thanks of an adulating crowd. While president Manuel Azaña and his prime minister Negrin both gave exalting speeches, it was the oration of a woman, Dolores Ibárruri, or La Pasionaria, which most captured the mood for posterity. Even doughty Scottish Brigaders were brought to tears by La Pasionaria's famously impassioned panegyric:

Comrades of the International Brigades! Political reasons, reasons of state, the good of that same cause for which you offered your blood with limitless generosity, send some of you back to your countries and some to forced exile. You can go with pride. You are history. You are legend. You are the heroic example of the solidarity and the universality of democracy. We will not forget you; and, when the olive tree of peace puts forth its leaves, entwined with the laurels of the Spanish Republic's victory, come back! Come back to us and here you will find a homeland.

In an unusually unrestrained outburst after hearing the speech, Peter Kerrigan wrote by way of reply:

Beloved, unconquerable Spanish brothers and sisters, we will come back to Spain some day to thank you all for all that you have taught us and to partake once more in happy circumstances of your boundless hospitality. Speed that day! Salud!

Bill Cranston too was overwhelmed by the parade and speech, remarking 'I really wanted to cry. We got a tremendous reception from the people of Barcelona and it's a thing I'll never forget, never.' George Murray was taken aback by the affection felt towards the Brigade: 'It was a very emotional sort of thing. Young girls were coming over and kissing you, all this kind of thing, which is surprising after all that time.'[31]

Sadly, the operators of international bureaucracy did not view the Brigaders with such reverence and it was another five weeks before they were allowed to leave Spain. Despite an International Commission having granted all of the men permission to leave a fortnight after the Barcelona parade, the frustrated members of the British Battalion were left to fester in a camp south of the French border. Willie Gallacher and a number of Labour and Liberal MPs raised the issue in parliament, while Brigade officials sent an urgent telegram to Clement Attlee demanding he press the matter with the prime minister Neville Chamberlain.

This pressure finally paid off. In the first week of December 1938, a train carrying 305 British Brigaders crossed the border into France, though only after it had initially broken down. On 7 December 1938, the train pulled into London Victoria, its war-weary passengers safely home. In London, Scottish Brigaders were provided with money for onward fares and food from the Co-operative and the International Brigade Association. Steve Fullarton travelled on a later train over the border with 68 other wounded Brigaders, leaving Spain on 21 December. So destitute was Fullarton, who had eaten a plate of ham and eggs on the border train and told the guard to charge the meal to Lord Halifax, the Royal Arsenal Co-operative provided him with a suit. A *Daily Worker* journalist relayed the reaction of Scottish Brigaders when they disembarked from the ferry in the Newhaven mist:

A Scottish voice reached me through the wind – 'Give me sunny Spain.' 'Aye, let's go back,' came another. They then made their way to their reserved carriages, some on stretchers. Tea with sugar was the first thing on their minds!

Sixteen of the wounded men were Scottish, and most had served in Spain for at least a year.

The communal praise heaped on the Brigaders by La Pasionaria and the people of Barcelona was echoed in Britain with a succession of welcome

British Battalion troops marching in early 1938. By the year's end, they had taken part in their final procession, through the streets of Barcelona.

receptions and rallies, though none were endorsed by the government as was the case in Spain. Robert Walker, Bob Cooney and token Englishman Sam Wild led their Battalion down the platform at Victoria Station and out into the street to a rapturous greeting from a crowd of 20,000. In his speech to those gathered, Cooney turned his attentions to the non-interventionist prime minister:

> The British Battalion is going into action against Chamberlain for the defence of Britain. We gave a pledge to the Spanish people that we would do everything in our power here in Britain to forward the cause of Spain, of democracy, of liberty.

Meanwhile, Willie Gallacher MP set out the challenge ahead:

> I speak on behalf of every section of the progressive movement in this country when I give you a welcome home. But a welcome home not to rest but to struggle harder than ever before to carry through to a conclusion the cause for which you have suffered so much.

Following the speeches, the Battalion, flanked by their audience, marched through London, laying a wreath on the Cenotaph for their fallen comrades, and delivering a petition to 10 Downing Street. Describing events, Tommy Bloomfield noted that the popular press were no more interested in praising the Brigade than they had been when he left for Spain:

When we arrived back in London we received no publicity except the report in the *Daily Worker*. The government wanted everything kept quiet. Sam Wild formed us into Battalion formation. He led us bearing our colours. He then placed our walking wounded in front of the Battalion marching on Downing Street. On reaching Downing Street a cordon of police halted us and said we could go no further. Our walking wounded split in two. Sam Wild marched through bearing our standard and told the inspector in charge that he was going to deliver our petition come hell or high water. The police didn't care to have the stigma of batoning wounded veterans of Spain so common sense prevailed and we were allowed to deliver our petition.

From London, 90 Scottish Brigaders boarded a bus bound for Glasgow on 11 December. They were met by another colossal crowd, who cheered the men, clad in khaki uniform, to the City Hall for an official reception. Scottish National Party Secretary John MacCormick spoke to the special guests and reaffirmed the message that the battle was not yet over:

Our comrades have returned from Spain and though they have laid down their arms the fight goes on – the fight for freedom without which there is no civilisation.

More laconically, Sir Hugh Robertson, conductor of Glasgow Orpheus Choir, commented, 'I want as a Scotsman to say "Aye, lads: I'm proud o' ye this day."' Bob Cooney once again mounted the podium and demonstrated that he had taken heart from the reaction the returning Brigaders had received:

We have met the real Britain in coming back. The Britain of whom we had experience in Spain made us furiously determined that we would have no rest until this rotten government is swept from office.

There was a certain amount of regret among Brigaders, as Thomas Quinn told a *Glasgow Herald* journalist:

In one way we are very glad to be home again and to see our friends here, but I think that all of us feel that we would like to have stayed on and to have fought the war to finish.

Returned Brigaders including Dundonian Arthur Nicoll (foreground, right) tour Britain in search of support for the Spanish republic.

Eight of the returnees travelled onwards by train to Edinburgh and yet more adulation. At Waverley station, a sizeable crowd awaited their arrival, as well as several councillors and key figures from the Edinburgh Trades and Labour Council, the CPGB and various trade unions. *The Scotsman* relayed details of their arrival:

> When the train arrived there were scenes touched with deep emotion on the platform when the men were welcomed by their relatives. The welcome they were given on the station roadways was loud and prolonged, the station ringing with the cheers of the crowd. The *'Internationale'* and the 'Red Flag' were sung and accompanied by band.

Behind banners of support, the eight and their followers walked on to the Free Gardeners' Hall in Picardy Place, where 'both the lower and upper halls were crowded for a welcoming meeting, at which the former members of the International Brigade gave brief speeches.'

In Dundee, a crowd welcomed seven returning Brigaders at the West Station on 12 December. Accompanied by a piper, the men led the crowd to a rally at the City Square, though the local Communist Party fell foul of Dundee Magistrates for failing to gain permission for the gathering. Such local red tape was unlikely to stop men who had fought at Jarama, Belchite and the Ebro.

Similar receptions were planned for the wounded arrivals, due in Scotland on the 23rd. Steve Fullarton and Jimmy Reid, neighbours in Shettleston and comrades in battle, were provided with lodgings in London for the night of the 22nd. That evening Reid, in Fullarton's words, 'decided he wanted his pint', and returned several hours later bearing news of a planned rendezvous the following day with a Glaswegian girl he had met. This would mean missing the 1pm train to Glasgow that Reid, Fullarton and Dusty Miller were booked onto. Miss it they did. At Glasgow Central a crowd had gathered, only to be left staring at the empty platform. Reid's pint had robbed the three of their moment of glory.

Once settled at home, Brigaders sometimes found reintegration into normal life difficult. Help was unlikely to come from a British government that had recognised Franco as Spain's sovereign leader in late February 1939, over a month before his conclusive victory. To emphasise their position, the Foreign Office sent out letters to all Brigaders to inform them

> that the sum of £3. 19. 3d. has been expended from public funds in connexion with your repatriation to the United Kingdom on evacuation from Spain. I am to request you to be good enough to refund this amount to this department.

Gratitude, indeed, for men who had tried to halt the march of European fascism – considerably earlier than the British state did. The reaction among Scottish Brigaders was uniform to each and every letter of final warning that arrived; in some areas of Glasgow, a wartime shortage of toilet paper was never likely. Tom Murray replied for hundreds of men when he wrote to the FO:

> I am sure it would not tax the resources of the British government to any greater extent to ignore my legal obligations, than it did to ignore its own legal obligations to supply the Spanish republic with arms and assistance.

Some letters arrived later than others; for Steve Fullarton, desperately trying to join the armed forces and once more stand up to Hitler and Mussolini, the timing was anything but impeccable:

> This was typical of the FO of the day. Get that fiver off him. Two days before the Battle of Britain. Can you imagine? People were talking about what we were going to do when the invasion came. I had it in my mind I would desert to the Highlands.

Fullarton, displaying a sense of decency that the government appeared to be bereft of, soon overcame his hurt and joined the Royal Air Force. This, despite the wartime need for military servants, proved to be a struggle; the Shettleston man was one of many Scots Brigaders who suffered from a covert system of blacklisting due to their service in Spain. In all, from initially volunteering to being presented with his uniform, it took Fullarton 14 months to join the RAF. He was made to gather extra references and came under an uncommon level of scrutiny. If he was in any doubt as to the reasoning behind this, all became clear when an officer in charge of recruitment barked at him 'Spain? Spain? You've been to Spain?!' and launched into a diatribe against the International Brigades. In the end, Fullarton's good character merited superlative references from his ex-employers and family doctor, though even the latter had to write 'He has been in Spain. If this is no bar to recruitment he is in every way suitable to the RAF.'

Tommy Bloomfield suffered a similar fate when trying to enlist with the Navy, asserting that 'we were victimised. When World War Two broke out I volunteered for the armed forces and was refused. No explanation was given.' After pressure from Willie Gallacher, Bloomfield was eventually permitted to serve.

Chris Smith, prior to becoming a Brigader a member of the Territorial Army, learned that the TA had banned those who served in Spain from joining or rejoining. Smith regularly found plain clothes police officers following and questioning him as to his political activities. Similarly, in 1967 George Drever was informed by Special Branch that each and every military and career role or promotion he had missed out on had been down to his involvement in Spain and his political beliefs.

As Drever had found, this blacklisting crossed over into the world of work. Tommy Bloomfield remained convinced until his dying day that his time in Spain had, in the eyes of others, left him unemployable:

As I had been a rigger in the Royal Navy, I applied for a job of work in Rosyth dockyard as a rigger knowing I could splice any wire rope up to two inches over my knee. Three times I applied and was informed there were no vacancies. Yet the man living next door to me was given work there. During the war he served in the RAF and was a Freemason. He could hardly walk with arthritis, he was blind in one eye and had a dicky heart. Good luck to him obtaining work. I needed work as well as him. But it seemed that as I had fought for democracy in Spain I must be a communist. I was fit to serve in the armed forces from 1939 to 1945 but not entitled to the right to work. If I'd fought for Franco I would have been given work.

Annie Murray still flying the flag half a century on.

They had gone from legendary status in Barcelona to pariah status in their own backyards.

Though ostracised by authority, not one Scottish Brigader displayed regret at his decision to go to Spain. All that Brigaders did rue was the eventual defeat of the republic, which most put down to Britain and France's non-interventionism and the assistance given to the nationalists by Germany and Italy. Neither were they bitter, though there was continuing widespread anger at the inaction of the British government. George Murray's pride was typical:

Looking back on the war after half a century, I would say the International Brigade was something unique. There was every nationality you could think of. I never had any regrets about what I did. My only regret was having a bullet through my chest. But no, no, I have no regrets. I'm quite proud of it.[32]

Tommy Bloomfield echoed Murray's sentiments, though added a sombre note about what the republican Spanish were left to face:

Looking back on my time in Spain I can only say I am both humble and proud to have known and served with the cream of the workers and the believers in true democracy. My heart goes to the workers of Spain for when Franco was victorious I can imagine the countless men and women who were slaughtered throughout the country simply for being anti-fascist.

The advent of the World War Two was something of a moral, if resolutely pyrrhic, victory for the Brigaders, many of whom, as we have seen, had warned that the failure to make Spain 'the tomb of fascism' would lead to wider conflict. Indeed, that wider war validated Brigaders' opinions that they were right to go and fight in Spain, as Bill Cranston averred:

I don't have any regrets about going to Spain. I would go back again if I was in the same position. I think the cause was a worthwhile one. What we said came true when Hitler started World War Two. He proved that we were right in what we said about the dangers from fascism.

As Roddy MacFarquhar put it:

We were convinced that if we could win we could stop war spreading. Had we been able to win we would have stopped Hitler and Mussolini in their tracks.

Predating historians in their analyses, Scottish Brigaders were among the first to postulate the now widely accepted opinion that the Spanish war was not a civil one. As David Anderson later suggested, 'it wasn't a civil war. It was a war of the Spanish people fighting for independence against fascism.'[33] Bob Cooney was of a similar opinion, and interestingly he even stated that in diverting Hitler's attentions and resources, the Spanish war had been a positive thing:

It was not a civil war. It was Hitler's and Mussolini's first round of the Second World War, and a costly round it proved for them. It can be truly said that the defeat of Hitler started in Spain. His timetable of aggression was dislocated for three years and the world was alerted to the nature of fascism by the destruction of Guernica and other atrocities.

Cooney was not alone in this viewpoint; Jimmy Maley felt that:

One good thing to come out of the Spanish war is that they stopped the German army starting the other war sooner than it did. It delayed the big war.

Despite the difficulties faced in joining the British armed forces, a majority of Scottish survivors of the war in Spain were to fight in that 'big war'. Many of the men were members of the CPGB, and by participating in World War Two they were defying the official instructions given by their Party, another representation of the absence of slavishness among Scots.

Donald Renton and John Londragan served in the Royal Artillery, while Eddie Brown served the Highland Light Infantry during the D-Day landings at Normandy. David Anderson and John Dunlop were in the Gordon Highlanders and Scots Guards respectively, and Bill Cranston served in Egypt for the duration of his five years in the army. Now experienced soldiers, many of the men excelled, although their political convictions were never far from the surface. Jimmy Maley, a member of the King's Own Scottish Borderers and then the Highland Light Infantry, served in Burma and India, where he became involved with communists recently released from prison and took part in a public debate on the causes of war with an army captain. Afterwards, Maley was given a prompt reproach by the military police.

Although now sporting the colours of a different conflict, after nearly a decade of war the British Battalion had played their part in finally defeating Hitler and Mussolini's fascism. To the chagrin of International Brigaders and exiled Spanish republicans, though, Franco's fascism was to remain as undisturbed by the Allied powers in 1945 as it had been in 1936. Their non-interventionism remained selective.

CHAPTER 17

'Something to be proud of': Conclusions

Today as a pensioner, I live on social security but I'm the richest man in this world having known my comrades of the International Brigades, and the leaders of the National Unemployed Workers' Movement along with the outstanding men and women of my era. If I had my life to live over again I would do the same as there is no other way.

Tommy Bloomfield

There are an amazing number of men from Scotland here, every day you meet someone from home so there is really no feeling of isolation for us.

Alec Park

ON 29 MARCH 1939, the city of Valencia became the last significant pocket of republican resistance to surrender. Franco's nationalists subsequently declared themselves to be the official government of Spain and an intense period of genocidal repression against republicans was instigated.

With the defeat of the republic came the defeat of a gargantuan Scottish effort that far outweighed the size or population of the country. Proportionally, Scotland sent more men to fight than anywhere else in Britain and arguably beyond. Nearly one third of them perished in Spain.

The aid movement mobilised on a scale not witnessed elsewhere. Scots, though suffering from some of the highest death rates and unemployment figures in Europe, gave time and money with boundless munificence.

Once in Spain, the Scottish contribution was similarly noteworthy. Scots were omnipresent in the highest ranks of the British Battalion. Wilfred McCartney, George Aitken, Jock Cunningham and Harold Fry all rose to become commanders of the Battalion. Cunningham, prior to his controversial expulsion from Spain, was lauded by the Brigades leadership and CPGB, none more so than in a speech made by Harry Pollitt at a Unity Campaign meeting in March 1937:

One day we shall tell our children about the defence of Madrid, this epic story that can never die in the pages of world history. I think of Jock Cunningham from Coatbridge out in Spain, the British Chapayev, leading his men fearlessly and unafraid, dancing with death. A word of encouragement here, over the top there, bringing in a wounded comrade here. Ceaselessly moving among his men until everyone has become influenced with the mighty unconquerable spirit of a worker blessed with a fiery hatred of capitalism and fascism. This is Jock Cunningham: our Chapayev.

Bob Cooney, who became Political Commissar to the entire British Battalion from April 1938 onwards, was similarly revered. Peter Kerrigan portrayed Cooney as

another about whose work it is impossible to speak too highly. Through the whole of his two months without a break of any kind and in every action, his steadiness has been a sheet anchor for others.

Tom Murray claimed that Cooney was 'more responsible than any other single individual for the splendid morale and military efficiency of the Bat-

One of many certificates awarded to Scottish Brigaders for their military accomplishments in Spain. This particular document records John Dunlop's efforts in the field of battle, particularly during the Ebro offensive, which merited his promotion from corporal to sergeant.

talion.' The Aberdonian was also immensely popular among regular Brigaders. Such was his devotion to them, he found himself at one point demoted to the role of rifleman for, said Brigades authorities, 'exhibiting "rank and filist" tendencies'. Scottish defiance of officialdom in Spain had surfaced once more.

As Political Commissar to the machine-gun company, Murray himself was one of many Scots who attained that position. Dundonian Arthur Nicoll achieved the feat of becoming commissar to the crack Anti-tank Unit, a company entirely separate from the British Battalion though containing a large Scottish contingent.

Nicoll and Murray were just two of the hundreds of Scots who received special citations from the republican authorities in Spain for their efforts. The latter was awarded a special certificate for his 'valour, enthusiasm, spirit of sacrifice and strong will power in the fight to crush fascism.' Prior to his death, George Jackson was made a corporal for his 'brave and determined work as a machine-gunner in very dangerous positions.' Bobby Walker was cited for 'coolness and efficiency in carrying through his task of Battalion Adjutant', and John Dunlop for being a 'glorious example of an anti-fascist fighter'.

Yet Scotland's greatest contribution to the war in Spain was not that of any individual. This was a collective, grassroots-up campaign unlike any seen since. Almost unanimously, the lion rampart roared on the Spanish republic. In the aid for Spain movement, working class women took a proactive rather than reactive political role for the first time ever. Politically, the energies of several interlinked movements were harnessed, providing a focal point for the 'red, red heart of the world' to rally around.

Though expressing his pride at being part of the International Brigades, Steve Fullarton could have been referring to pro-republican Scotland in its entirety when he movingly said:

Here were a body of men who I don't think will ever be equalled in their intensity of purpose, trying to eliminate fascism. There are many people who set out on different jobs and they fall by the wayside. But not them. And that's been my pride, that I was one of them. That's something to be proud of.

While it may appear that the cases of Bob Smillie and Ethel MacDonald were what exported Spain's war to Scotland, in truth the Scottish people had already made the republic's struggle their own. They had paid homage *from* Caledonia. It was truly a glorious, if often tragic, chapter in Scotland's unwritten history.

Interviews and Printed Material Quoted

1. All George Watters quotes courtesy of notes of an interview by Ian MacDougall, a form of which appeared in *Voices*, from NLS Acc. 11526
2. Interview with Donald Renton conducted by Victor Kiernan
3. Interview with George Murray in MacDougall, *Voices* p. 101
4. Interview with Jimmy Maley on BBC Radio Scotland, 17 November 2006
5. *Blue Blanket*, an early 1950s magazine by the Cultural Committee of the Edinburgh Communist Party
6. Interview with Donald Renton conducted by Victor Kiernan
7. Interview with Donald Renton conducted by Victor Kiernan
8. Interview with George Murray in MacDougall, *Voices* p. 101
9. Interview with Donald Renton conducted by Victor Kiernan
10. Interview with Jimmy Maley on BBC Radio Scotland, 17 November 2006
11. Interview with Donald Renton conducted by Victor Kiernan
12. In Rust, *Britons in Spain* p. 24
13. Interview with John Dunlop in *The Scotsman*, 17 July 1996
14. Interview with Donald Renton conducted by Victor Kiernan
15. Interview with Donald Renton conducted by Victor Kiernan
16. Funeral reading by Murdoch Taylor, 17 May 1987
17. Interview with George Murray in MacDougall, *Voices* p. 102
18. Interview with Roddy MacFarquhar in MacDougall, *Voices* p. 82
19. Interview with Annie Murray in MacDougall, *Voices* p. 69
20. Interview with Annie Murray in MacDougall, *Voices* p. 74
21. Booklet commemorating Fife International Brigaders, 1983
22. All James Miller quotations from a booklet commemorating Fife International Brigaders, 1983
23. Interview with Tom Clarke in MacDougall, *Voices* p. 67. Other estimates put the number closer to 60
24. www.spanishrefugees-basquechildren.org
25. Orwell, George, *Homage to Catalonia*. All quotations taken from 1938 edition (London: Secker and Warburg, 1938), p.48 and p. 292
26. Interview with Hugh Sloan in MacDougall, *Voices* p. 217
27. Interview with Tom Murray in MacDougall, *Voices* p. 329
28. John Dunlop quotes in chapter 14 courtesy of MacDougall, *Voices* pp. 117–68
29. Interview with Tom Murray in MacDougall, *Voices* p. 318
30. Interview with Bob Cooney in *The Road to Spain*, p. 121
31. Interview with George Murray in MacDougall, *Voices* p. 104
32. Interview with George Murray in MacDougall, *Voices* p. 104
33. Interview with David Anderson in MacDougall, *Voices* p. 93

Archival Sources

I have avoided repetitious footnoting and referencing for obviously archival, unpublished and interview content referenced in the main text body. I have applied the same system for newspaper quotes. I am indebted to the Marx Memorial Library and the National Library of Scotland for the vast bulk of quoted unpublished material in the book (for exact references, see the Bibliography section). Published data used has been acknowledged in Endnote form. The quoted material from interviews conducted with Donald Renton by Victor Kiernan, from the Inter-University Consortium Film: *The Spanish Civil War*, are reproduced with the permission of Owen Dudley Edwards and Paul Addison.

University of Edinburgh, Department of History

Professor VG Kiernan – interviews with John Dunlop, Donald Renton and George Watters

National Library of Scotland

Acc. 7914–7915   David Murray papers
Acc. 9083   Tom, Anne and George Murray papers
Acc. 10042   John Lennox papers
Acc. 10043   David Anderson and John Londragan papers
Acc. 11479   John Gollan papers
Acc. 11526   Ian MacDougall papers
Acc. 12087   John Dunlop papers

Marx Memorial Library: International Brigade Archive

1986 Catalogue

Box 1: C/18a; Box 21: File F; Box 33a: Book 12, Sheets 1–6; Box 34: File A; Box 34: File B; Box 40: File B; Box 44: All; Box 45: All; Box 50: File AK; Box 50: File DN; Box 50: File FL; Box 50: File GL; Box 50: File McA; Box 50: File McC; Box 50: File McG; Box 50: File McW; Box 50: File Mi; Box 50: File My; Box 50: File Wi/17; Box 50: File Wi/18; Box 50: File Wi/23; Box 50: File Wi/35; Box 50: File Wi/40; Box 50: File Wi/59; Box 50: File Wi/66; Box 50: File Wk

1990 Catalogue

Boxes A – 2,3 & 4: File A; File C; File S/39

Box A – 12: File Bro; File Ke; File McC; File Pa; File Ru; File SL; File Sm; File Wk
Box A – 15: 3 (Cooney)
Box B – 4: File Q; File R
Box B – 6; File J

1994 Catalogue

Box C: File 1/4; File 1/4c; File 1/5; File 5/5; File 6/1; File 10; File 11/2; File 13/2; File 13/3; File 14/3; File 17/7; File 23; File 24; File 25; File 26
Box D – 1: File D
Box D – 3: File D
Box D – 4: File My; File Tn/1
Box D – 7: File A/2

Select Bibliography

Books

Baxell, Richard *British Volunteers in the Spanish Civil War*. Abersychan: Warren and
Pell, 2007

Beevor, Antony *The Battle for Spain*. London: Weidenfeld & Nicolson, 2006

Bell, Adrian *Only for Three Months: The Basque Children in Exile*. Norwich:
Mousehold Press, 1996

Buchanan, Tom *Britain and the Spanish Civil War*. Cambridge: Cambridge
University Press, 1997

Corkhill, David and Stuart Rawnsley (eds) *The Road to Spain: Anti-fascists at War*.
Dunfermline: Borderline Press, 1981

Fyrth, Jim *The Signal was Spain*. London: Lawrence and Wishart, 1986

Keene, Judith *Fighting for Franco*. London: Leicester University Press, 2001

MacDougall, Ian (ed) *Voices from the Spanish Civil War*. Edinburgh: Polygon, 1986

Orwell, George *Homage to Catalonia*. London: Secker and Warburg, 1938

Rust, Bill *Britons in Spain*. Abersychan: Warren and Pell, 2003

Spark, Muriel *The Prime of Miss Jean Brodie*. London: Penguin Classics, 2000

Maley, John and Maley, Willy *From the Calton to Catalonia*, Glasgow City
Libraries, 1992

Newspapers and journals

Barcelona Bulletin, 1937
Bellshill Speaker, 1937
Blue Blanket, 1952
Catholic Herald and Glasgow Observer, 1936–39
Forward, 1937
Frente Rojo, 1937
La Politica, 1937
New Leader, 1936–39
Regeneracion, 1936
Save Spain, Act Now!, 1939
Scottish Labour History, volume 34 (1999), and volume 37 (2002)
The Daily Mail, 1936–39
The Daily Express, 1936–39
The Daily Worker, 1936–39
The Glasgow Herald, 1936–39
The Glasgow Evening Times, 1936–39
The Scotsman, 1936–39
The Sunday Mail, 1936–39

Index

Luath Press Limited
committed to publishing well written books worth reading

LUATH PRESS takes its name from Robert Burns, whose little collie
Luath (*Gael.*, swift or nimble) tripped up Jean Armour at a wedding
and gave him the chance to speak to the woman who was to be his wife
and the abiding love of his life. Burns called one of the 'Twa Dogs'
Luath after Cuchullin's hunting dog in Ossian's *Fingal*.
Luath Press was established in 1981 in the heart of
Burns country, and is now based a few steps up
the road from Burns' first lodgings on
Edinburgh's Royal Mile. Luath offers you
distinctive writing with a hint of
unexpected pleasures.
Most bookshops in the UK, the US, Canada,
Australia, New Zealand and parts of Europe,
either carry our books in stock or can order them
for you. To order direct from us, please send a £sterling
cheque, postal order, international money order or your
credit card details (number, address of cardholder and
expiry date) to us at the address below. Please add post
and packing as follows: UK – £1.00 per delivery address;
overseas surface mail – £2.50 per delivery address; overseas airmail
– £3.50 for the first book to each delivery address, plus £1.00 for each
additional book by airmail to the same address. If your order is a gift,
we will happily enclose your card or message at no extra charge.

Luath Press Limited
543/2 Castlehill
The Royal Mile
Edinburgh EH1 2ND
Scotland
Telephone: +44 (0)131 225 4326 (24 hours)
Fax: +44 (0)131 225 4324
email: sales@luath. co.uk
Website: www. luath.co.uk